Elite • 157

The German Home Front 1939–45

Brian L Davis • Illustrated by Malcolm McGregor

Consultant editor Martin Windrow

First published in Great Britain in 2007 by Osprey Publishing,
Midland House, West Way, Botley, Oxford OX2 0PH, UK
443 Park Avenue South, New York, NY 10016, USA

E-mail: info@ospreypublishing.com

A CIP catalogue record for this book is available from the British Library

ISBN 978 1 84603 185 4

Editor: Martin Windrow
Page layouts by Ken Vail Graphic Design, Cambridge, UK
Typeset in Helvetica Neue and ITC New Baskerville
Index by Glyn Sutcliffe
Originated by PPS Grasmere, Leeds, UK
Printed in China through World Print Ltd.

07 08 09 10 11   10 9 8 7 6 5 4 3 2 1

A CIP catalogue record for this book
is available from the British Library

FOR A CATALOGUE OF ALL BOOKS PUBLISHED BY OSPREY MILITARY AND
AVIATION PLEASE CONTACT:

NORTH AMERICA
Osprey Direct, c/o Random House Distribution Center, 400 Hahn Road,
Westminster, MD 21157
E-mail: info@ospreydirect.com

ALL OTHER REGIONS
Osprey Direct UK, P.O. Box 140 Wellingborough, Northants, NN8 2FA, UK
E-mail: info@ospreydirect.co.uk

Buy online at www.ospreypublishing.com

Acknowledgements

The author is most grateful to Malcolm McGregor for his
excellent artwork; to Frederick Walker and Alex Vanags, for
assistance with translations and also providing answers to
technical questions regarding life in wartime Germany. Both
author and artist wish to acknowledge particularly the
assistance afforded by Herr Hartmut Schlüter,
Museumsleitung of *Feuer.Wehrk*, the Feueurwehrmuseum at
Hattingen, Germany.

Photographic credit

Unless otherwise credited all images are from the author's
collection.

Artist's note

I would like to take the opportunity to thank the following
for their help and support during the preparation of the
artwork for this book. Firstly, to Brian Davis, for unfettered
access to his unique and invaluable reference collection. To
Andrew Cormack, FSA, of the RAF Museum, Hendon, for
the opportunity to take detailed photographs of a German
gas mask. As too often in the past, to the staff of the
Imperial War Museum, Lambeth. Finally, to Anne for her
much-needed support and encouragement.

Readers may care to note that the original paintings from
which the colour plates in this book were prepared are
available for private sale. All reproduction copyright
whatsoever is retained by the Publishers. All enquiries
should be addressed to:

Malcolm McGregor,
64 Cavendish Avenue,
Ealing,
London,
W13 0QJ,
UK

The Publishers regret that they can enter into no
correspondence upon this matter.

**TITLE PAGE A mixed group of uniformed personnel,
including troops and (right) an NCO of the Fire
Protection Police, help in search and clearance work
after an air raid. Scenes such as this were enacted
throughout Germany in the years 1942–45, and
became almost a daily routine in the major cities.**

THE GERMAN HOME FRONT 1939-45

INTRODUCTION

To understand the conditions of life in Germany between 1 September 1939, when Germany invaded Poland, and 8 May 1945, when the German nation capitulated to the victorious Allied forces, it is essential to appreciate the way in which the National Socialist German Workers Party (the Nazi Party, NSDAP) imposed repressive laws, decrees and regulations on the German people from within a few weeks of their gaining power in early 1933. This progressive pre-war legislation, much of it driven by Nazi ideology and all of it intended to destroy any popular or institutional focus for opposition to the regime, had a profound effect on every sphere of civilian life.

The collection of money for the relief of German citizens during the winter months, the Winterhilfswerk des Deutschen Volkes, was an annual pre-war event; here, a small boy dressed as a policeman holds a collecting tin while standing on a tank with a Panzer soldier. During the wartime years the emphasis of the renamed Kriegswinterhilfswerk shifted to providing German troops, particularly those fighting on the Eastern Front, with comforts; leading Nazi officials occasionally appeared in public with a collecting tin to persuade passers-by to make a contribution. The appeal for donations of warm clothing for the troops in Russia in December 1941 met with a generous response, but caused great surprise and disillusion that such an *ad hoc* measure should be necessary – especially as it coincided with several unexplained dismissals among senior field commanders.

Those regulations introduced from 1939, out of actual or ostensible wartime necessity, inflicted further restrictions and difficulties on an already burdened population. The war itself naturally brought increasing shortages and hardships; millions suffered personal separations and bereavements, and great disruption of their domestic and working lives. Civilians living in all but remote rural areas faced an increasing ordeal under Allied aerial bombardment, and millions were made homeless. However, although the air raids caused devastation and exhaustion, the emergency services and civil administration continued to operate; industry proved remarkably resilient, and in the intervals between air raids what passed for normal life resumed as best it could. But in the final months of the war the civilian population were confronted by the advance of Allied forces towards and into Germany; and when defeat, surrender and occupation by the enemy became imminent, they were left to fend for themselves, their chances of survival dependent on the behaviour of the occupying troops. In the East, huge numbers of civilians continued to lose their lives long after the official ceasefire, and millions were driven from their homes.

The manipulation of public attitudes by propaganda was a major feature of the Nazi state. This was broadly successful when it paralleled natural feelings of patriotism; but in particular instances it often failed to achieve the desired results – especially when it underestimated the public's intelligence, or worked against the grain of normal human emotions. Surviving documents include the reports of Security Service (SD) agents and informers, down to the everyday level of conversations overheard in streets, shops and air-raid shelters. These reveal a steady loss of respect for the Nazi Party, due to the failure of its officials to live up to the ideals they were proclaiming and the sacrifices they were demanding of their fellow-citizens. Until almost the very end, however, respect for Adolf Hitler himself remained high; a constant refrain was 'if only the Führer knew about these scandals, he would soon sort them out.'[1]

THE NATIONAL SOCIALIST STATE

The Nazi Party attained power on 30 January 1933 with the appointment of Adolf Hitler as Reichskanzler (National Chancellor – broadly, prime minister) by the senile President von Hindenburg. A few weeks later an attempt to burn down the Reichstag (parliament building), probably by a deranged Dutch Communist, provided the excuse for harsh measures against the Communist and Social Democratic parties. On 28 February 1933, Hindenburg signed a decree 'for the suppression of Communist acts of violence endangering the German State'. This decree suspended the articles of the constitution that guaranteed the liberty of the person, the freedom of the press and the right of assembly (free trade unions would be simply abolished two months later). It permitted the police to make house searches and to confiscate documents or property at will.

[1] For readers seeking more information than can possibly even be summarized in a book of this size, a rich source of detailed material and statistics on many aspects of government and life in wartime Germany is published in Britain by the University of Exeter Press (1998): *Nazism 1919–45 – A Documentary Reader: Vol 4, The German Home Front in World War II*, ed. Jeremy Noakes, ISBN 0 85989 311 1. A less academic and highly illustrated social study is also recommended: *The German Home Front 1939–45* by Terry Charman (Barrie & Jenkins, London, 1989; ISBN 0 7126 2183 0)

Parades were regularly held in Berlin and other major cities, to mark anniversaries of important dates in the Party's calendar or to celebrate military victories. These photos of Hitler's annual birthday parade on 20 April – here, his 50th, in 1939 – give an idea of the size of these displays and of the vast crowds of spectators.

The Reich government was empowered to take over the administration of any Länder (the regions of Germany, partly self-governing under the Weimar Constitution) which did not take measures to carry out government intentions, and the death penalty was introduced for a wide range of crimes.

The Nazi Party gained 44 per cent of the votes in the last multi-party election on 5 March 1933, and on 20 March the details of an Enabling Bill were released. This law was ostensibly to remain in force until 1 April 1937, or until the Communists ceased to constitute any danger to the State. In reality this 'temporary, emergency' measure provided the foundation for the powers wielded by the regime throughout the 12-year life of the Third Reich; and from the moment this law was passed, no German had any right of appeal against any government measure.

One of the most visible faces of the Nazi state was Dr Josef Goebbels (right, in leather coat). Apart from his ministerial powers as, effectively, the controller of public knowledge and of many other aspects of domestic affairs, he held the parallel Party post of Gauleiter of Berlin. In this capacity he frequently visited areas damaged by air raids and talked to both victims and emergency workers – as here, after the raid of 30/31 March 1943. Hitler, by contrast, became less and less visible, shunning contact with the ordinary people whose lives were devastated by his war. Nevertheless, many Germans retained their faith in the Führer long after they had become cynical about the Party and the regime as a whole.

The Reichstag empowered the government to legislate on any subject, to decree the budget, to alter the constitution, and to ratify treaties. Most importantly, Hitler, as Chancellor, was to promulgate the laws instead of the President; the legislative rights of parliament and of the presidency fell into abeyance, the latter losing all its functions except that of head of the armed forces. In the meantime the cabinet could suspend the independence of the judiciary, and administer the finances without making public the budget (and thus, expenditure on the armed forces and security apparatus). The regime could, in fact, do anything it chose except actually abolishing outright the now-impotent parliament (the Reichstag and Reichsrat).

On the death of President von Hindenburg in August 1934, Hitler assumed the leadership of both Party and State as Führer (Leader) – a decision endorsed by 38 million Germans in a plebiscite. Thereafter the unfettered Nazi leadership increased the pace of their organization of the German state on a highly centralized basis. The political, economic and cultural life of the country, the police, the courts, education, the media and every aspect of the administration were directly controlled from Berlin, by-passing regional and local administrations. In 1935 the so-called Nuremberg Laws enshrined Nazi racial ideology, depriving Jewish Germans of their citizenship rights and introducing strict new marriage laws (see below, 'The Persecution of Jews in Germany').

The regime also began a more stealthy persecution of active members of the Protestant and Roman Catholic churches, to remove their considerable popular influence; the official line is summed up by the pronouncement in February 1937 by Hans Kerrl, Reich Minister for Religious Affairs, that 'To us now is risen the incarnation of what Christianity really is – Adolf Hitler!' The Party never succeeded in stamping out religious observance, and as the war turned against Germany church-going actually increased. The mass of church-going people – particularly in rural areas – remained stubbornly faithful; for instance, when the government banned religious holidays they simply took days off from work to attend the traditional ceremonies. Among many instances of courageous resistance to the Nazis by churchmen, one example is Bishop von Galen of Munster, who in August 1941 denounced from the pulpit the euthanasia programme (see 'Public Health', below); this was discontinued soon afterwards.

Administration

On 30 August 1939 the Ministerial Council for the Defence of the State was established, composed of six leading Nazis closest to Hitler.[2] From the outbreak of war the Council bore a large measure of responsibility for the actual guidance of the Reich economy and administration, enacting laws and issuing decrees without being bound by existing legislation. However, it should be noted that the Nazi power structure – both before and after the outbreak of war – was far from monolithic or even closely integrated.

Hitler ruled by making broad pronouncements, leaving their implementation to his highly competitive lieutenants. The lines of demarcation between the powers and responsibilities of these rival courtiers were often unclear, overlapping or contradictory; individuals made continual attempts to capture the Führer's ear (usually via his gatekeeper Martin Bormann, the Party chief), and to persuade him to make some response that could be presented as endorsing their particular programmes and ambitions. Below these leading personalities, their subordinates at many levels indulged in self-seeking bureaucratic 'empire-building', to the detriment of the national war effort.

In theory, 17 ministries operated the administration of the Reich: (1) Interior, (2) Foreign Affairs, (3) Public Enlightenment & Propaganda, (4) Press, (5) Finance, (6) Police, (7) Justice, (8) Economic Affairs, (9) Food & Agriculture, (10) Labour, (11) Armaments & War Production, (12) Science & Education, (13) Religious Affairs, (14) Transport, (15) Post & Telegraph, (16) High Command of the Armed Forces, (17) Air. Each of these was headed by a minister assisted by one or more under-secretaries. Ministries were sub-divided into departments (Abteilungen) usually under a Ministerial Director (Ministerialdirektor). These were in turn separated into sections (Unterabteilungen) headed by sub-directors

The militarization of German society extended to the mass of workers. One of the Nazis' first acts on gaining power was to abolish free trade unions on 2 May 1933, sequestering their funds for the new Deutsches Arbeitsfront (German Work Front, DAF). Here uniformed members parade with flags in the Ehrenhof or forecourt of the new State Chancellery. The DAF was a nation-wide Party organization, headed by Dr Robert Ley; membership was compulsory for all workers who were racially and politically acceptable, and by 1939 the membership was reported as 22.4 million – some 28 per cent of the entire population.

---

[2] Göring (Chairman), Hess (Deputy Führer), Frick (Administration), Funk (Economy), Lammers (Head of Chancellery), Keitel (Head of Armed Forces High Command, OKW). Other members could from time to time be co-opted on to the Ministerial Council by the chairman.

(Ministerialdirigenten). The staffs of these component parts of the ministries comprised ministerial councillors (Ministerialräte) and other officials and civil servants.

However, even before the outbreak of the war special provision had been made for the completely centralized control demanded by the Nazis. The last meeting of the actual cabinet was in November 1937, and thereafter there was no formal machinery for co-ordinating the work of the ministries. Instead, a Commissioner-General for Reich Administration received broad powers for the co-ordination of administration throughout the Reich, and a Commissioner-General for Economic Affairs was given similar authority in that sphere. An elaborate Office for the Four-Year Plan was given far-reaching powers over many of the existing administrative agencies in the field of industry. Other special authorities – e.g. the Commissioner for War Production, and the Inspector-Generals of German Roads, Motor Transport, and Water and Power – were also superimposed upon the existing ministries, through which they acted.

It is not easy for citizens of modern democracies to appreciate fully the integration of the governmental structure of the German Reich with that of the National Socialist Party. As in post-war Communist and other one-party dictatorships, the links were so complete that it was difficult to determine, in many instances, what was Government and what was Party. In general terms, the Party had a national organization that paralleled the government structure, and in large measure controlled it down to the lowest levels; the heads of the Party agencies very often held corresponding offices in the government. In the simplest practical terms, during much of the war the Home Front was ruled by Bormann (the Party chief), Goebbels (information, propaganda, and a whole wider field of civil affairs), Himmler (police and repression) and Speer (war production).

One of the final aspects of the Party's control was the creation in October 1944 of the Deutsche Volkssturm (German People's Assault Force), a Home Guard militia of boys from 16 years old who had not yet been conscripted for the Wehrmacht, and of men up to the age of 60. The Volkssturm was envisaged by Himmler, Bormann and Goebbels as a force for heroic, last-ditch defence of the Reich; it was organized and trained by the SA, NSKK and SS, and controlled by regional Party officials as part of the Replacement Army headed by Reichsführer-SS Himmler. In fact its enthusiasm for self-sacrifice was – naturally enough – even less impressive than its rag-bag of uniforms and weapons. These are members of a unit captured by US troops at Juchen, west of the Rhine; some wear the insignia of Customs officials.

The Party leadership structure

The highest level of the Party was formed by the Reichsleitern, 17 of whom held state positions; each Reichsleiter (national leader) was responsible to Adolf Hitler as President, Chancellor and Leader of the Nazi Party. The NSDAP structure was based on the 42 Gaue (regions) of the Greater German Reich. Each Gau was headed by a Gauleiter (regional leader), and his area of administration was in turn divided into a number of Kreise or 'circles' each controlled by a Kreisleiter (district leader) – the lowest of the paid appointments. Beneath the Kreisleiter were the unpaid Ortsgruppenleitern (local group leaders); each of these was responsible for an Ortsgruppe with, on average, a population of about 40,000 people – one or several 'communes' or, within a large town, a certain district. The Ortsgruppen were the smallest units in rural areas; in large metropolitan centres they were sub-divided into Zellen (street cells) and Blöcke (blocks) led by Party volunteers of the lowest ranks. Cell leaders (Zellenleiter) controlled four or five Blöcke, and block leaders (Blockleiter) were responsible for 40 to 60 households – on whose members they kept careful card-index records.

In December 1943 the Party claimed that membership was 6,500,000 male members incuding 85,800 full-time officials.

12 July 1943: citizens of Cologne are decorated by a senior Party official, believed to be the Gauleiter of Gau 12 (Köln-Aachen), Josef Grohè. Note the special Party armband with golden oakleaves – see also Plate A2 for the Party uniform of senior functionaries.

LAW AND THE PENAL SYSTEM

The Nazi regime abandoned previous German legal traditions, and increasingly employed the codified laws as weapons of domination; resistance to this process by elements in the judiciary was virtually overcome after the death of Justice Minister Franz Gürtner in February 1941. Much legislation was promulgated by the Nazis in an *ad hoc* way, in the form of decrees and administrative instructions (or even simply in speeches and letters uttered and issued by Hitler and his senior henchmen).

From before the outbreak of war the State Justice Ministry came under increasingly successful pressure to yield its prerogatives over prosecution and sentencing to the SS/SD apparatus; equally, members of the Party and security agencies themselves enjoyed increasing immunity from prosecution. The ordinary courts were deprived of jurisdiction over growing areas of the legal codes; 'Special Courts' and 'People's Courts' were created as early as 1934, with greatly accelerated and simplified procedures, and extraordinary powers in 'political' matters – these being defined by almost infinitely elastic criteria.

Compared with Great Britain or the USA (even under wartime emergency powers), the 'rule of law' as we understand the concept no longer existed. The overriding function of the system was, in the simplest terms, to eliminate political resistance or criminal activity which

Juvenile crime

This poster, exhorting the Hitler Youth to join the air-raid protection service, echoes the popular image of German wartime adolescents. But teenagers are teenagers everywhere; many rebelled against the conformity of their elders, and hung around in groups to smoke, drink, listen to music, dance, and explore their sexuality. The Nazi authorities cracked down angrily on such 'anti-social' practices, and members of several particularly visible 'gangs' ended up doing hard labour in prison.

The 'Edelweiss Pirates' originated in the industrial Rhineland; they recognized each other by an Edelweiss or other badge under the left lapel. (Interestingly, when they were in HJ uniform they often flaunted these badges openly – including skull symbols, which may thus be completely misinterpreted in photographs). They favoured longer hairstyles, check shirts, short trousers, and white socks, pullovers and scarves. These working-class teenagers sometimes took serious risks; they sheltered deserters and escapees, and on one occasion even attacked the chief of the Cologne Gestapo – for which several were hanged in public in November 1944.

Youngsters of the more prosperous classes, particularly around Hamburg in the north, called themselves 'Swing Kids' after their passion for US and British music. They styled their clothes on an idea of British fashions – long tweed jackets and rolled umbrellas (!); identified themselves by a fancy collar stud in the lapel; and greeted each other with 'Heil Benny' (for the American bandleader Benny Goodman). The Swing Kids seldom got into any worse trouble than scrapping with HJ street patrols – few would risk fighting the Police.

Absolutely distinct were the few serious political activists, such as the famous White Rose group of students which formed around Professor Kurt Huber at Munich University. Led by Sophie and Hans Scholl, they were arrested for scattering anti-Nazi leaflets in 1942–43 and, after interrogation under torture, were beheaded in February 1943.

might undermine the power of the regime or the solidarity and efficiency of the nation at war. New offences were created, often in deliberately vague language, and a collective legal concept of offender types (e.g. 'national pests') reduced the judges' freedom over sentencing. Judges came under great pressure to give less importance to whether or not a particular law had actually been broken than to the alleged wider effects of the defendants' behaviour, and to pass the sentences desired by the regime. A catch-all offence of 'undermining the war effort' became a capital crime as early as August 1939; and the use of the death penalty by the courts (quite apart from killings in the concentration camps) increased from, e.g., 38 death sentences in 1938 to 5,336 in 1943. When the courts failed to pass sufficiently harsh sentences these were liable to be 'corrected' after the SS claimed custody of the convict. From September 1942, even persistent petty criminals were classed as 'anti-social elements' (alongside Jews, gypsies, and foreign labourers convicted of crimes) who might be handed over to the SS, explicitly to be worked to death in the concentration camps, where few survived for more than a few months.

Prisons

The ordinary criminal prison system was administered by Department V of the Ministry of Justice, which gave orders directly to the officials in charge of local institutions. Intermediate control on matters of supervision of sentences, personnel, etc., was exercised by the Generalstaatsanwälte (prosecutors) attached to the Oberlandesgerichte (courts of appeal). The ordinary prison system was run by civil servants trained in penology but also subject to Nazi control. The types of prisons included the following:

Arbeitshaus – for the 'educational' detention of vagrants, prostitutes, etc after service of sentence.

Haftanstalt - for the punishment of minor offences (Übertretungen).

Jugendarrestanstalt – for punishment of juveniles.

Sicherungsanstalt – for detention of habitual or dangerous criminals after service of sentence.

Strafanstalt/Strafgefängnis – conventional adult prison.

Zuchthaus – for adults sentenced to penal servitude (hard labour).

Untersuchungsgefängnis/Untersuchungshaftanstalt – remand prisons attached to courts for detention of accused pending trial; also used for prisoners serving short sentences for minor crimes.

Concentration camps

This book cannot attempt even to summarize the 'Final Solution' – the Holocaust – which was committed largely in the extermination camps situated on captured territory rather than in Germany itself. However, since the concentration camps within Germany long pre-dated the Holocaust, the following brief notes are in order.

At any time throughout the 12-year period of the Third Reich the Nazis interned hundreds of thousands of Germans in administrative detention, always under conditions of great physical hardship, without sufficient food, and subject to arbitrary violence up to and including death in custody. In 1933–36, while the regime was still consolidating its grip, these were mainly political and ideological opponents – Communists, Socialists, and Jews who were politically or culturally active, such as journalists. A minority of these were actually released after serving determinate sentences. After that period the net was cast wider, to sweep in anybody the regime demonized as being 'outside the national community' – habitual criminals, homosexuals, gypsies, members of sects such as the Jehovah's Witnesses, or anyone else who was deemed to threaten the solidarity of the Volk through racial origin or any failure to abide by the norms of National Socialist Germany. Vast numbers of these prisoners were detained indefinitely without specific charge, and many

Dachau, opened on 20 March 1933 just outside the city of Munich, was the first of a number of pre-war concentration camps. These were places for harsh internment, brutal punishment and 'correction'; outright extermination camps were to come later – but nevertheless, the records of Buchenwald camp show that in 1939 there were 9,553 new arrivals and no less than 1,235 deaths. Here, at Sachsenhausen camp, SS officials (left) answer the questions of Prof Landra, leader of the Italian Race-Political Department. Note the red-on-yellow triangles making a Star-of-David patch on the prisoners' jackets; these identified Jewish prisoners at that date. Red triangles identified political prisoners; green, habitual criminals; black, 'anti-social' elements; pink, homosexuals, and violet, Jehovah's Witnesses.

A Hauptwachtmeister of the Schutzpolizei (compare Plate G2) supervises the fixing of a sign showing the way to the nearest open public air raid shelter. His smart uniform and bearing remind us of the paramilitary nature and high public status of German police even before the Nazis came to power. (Courtesy Josef Charita)

others for imaginary offences used to cloak their detention for political reasons. However, the camps also held a proportion of ordinary criminals, military delinquents and non-Germans. A few special camps existed for women.

Concentration camps were under the direct control of the Reichsführer-SS Heinrich Himmler, through the Commander of Concentration Camps (Kommandeur der Konzentrationslager) and the Inspector of Death's-Head Units (Inspekteur der Totenkopf-Verbände), both senior members of the SS Central Office. The Inspector of Death's-Head Units was responsible for the guarding and security of the camps; their general administration came under the SS War Economy & Administration Headquarters (Wehrwirtschaft und Verwaltungs-Hauptamt). This apparent anomaly is explained by the fact that the SS ran the camps as a business; for instance, as early as 1938 the SS established a quarrying company, and soon inmate labour – either for SS-front companies, or hired out to industry – was bringing in millions of marks for Himmler's empire. Commandants of concentration camps headed staffs drawn from the SS; a political officer (Kommissar) had authority to release or otherwise dispose of inmates. Groups of prisoners were organized under a Lagerältester (a senior prisoner), with subordinate grades of Blockführer, Zugführer, Stubenältester, and Vorarbeiter; these so-called 'Kapos' were frequently ordinary criminals specially selected for their brutality and encouraged by petty privileges.

THE POLICE

The right to exercise police powers was transferred, in January 1934, from the regional Länder to the state (Reich). The process of centralization culminated in the creation in April 1934 of the post of Chef der Deutschen Polizei im Reichsministerium des Innern (Chief of the German Police in the Reich Ministry of the Interior), held by Heinrich Himmler as National Leader of the SS.[3]

The police authorities existed at three administrative levels. The Landespolizeibehörde (regional police authority) was the level immediately below the Headquarters of the Order Police in Berlin. It was headed in Prussia and Bavaria by the Regierungspräsident, and in other Länder by variously titled officials. Subordinate to the Landespolizeibehörde was the Kreispolizeibehörde (county or city police authority), headed in the Landkreis by the Landrat, in the Stadtkreis by the Oberbürgermeister, and in cities or in districts under direct National Police Administration by the Staatliche Polizeiverwalter (national police administrator). Subordinate to the Kreispolizeibehörde was the Ortspolizeibehörde, which existed in small communities in which the mayor usually headed the police authority.

[3] For fuller details, see also Men-at-Arms 434: *World War II German Police Units*

Shortly after Heinrich Himmler's appointment as Chief of the German Police in April 1934, he divided the existing police into two main sections under rigid national control: the Sicherheitspolizei (Security Police, Sipo) and the Ordnungspolizei (Order Police, Orpo). The functions of the German police widely exceeded those of other national police forces, and various police organizations concerned themselves with almost every area of the German citizen's life.

The Ordnungspolizei

The Order Police was the uniformed service. The Hauptamt Ordnungspolizei (Head Office of the Order Police) directed the following distinct forces:

(a) Schutzpolizei (Protection Police, Schupo), consisting of the following:

Schutzpolizei des Reichs – employed in cities and districts under National Police Administration. They included the Traffic Police (*Verkehrsbereitschaften*); and the Barrack Police (*Kasernierte Polizei*), the latter a highly trained militarized reserve equipped with armoured cars and heavy weapons, deployed if need be to mass demonstrations, severe air raids or similar emergencies.

Schutzpolizei der Gemeinden (Municipal Police) – the local police forces in communities outside the National Police Administration.

Verkehrskompanien (*mot*) *zbV* (Motorized Special Duty Traffic Police) – to patrol the main highways, regulate traffic and enforce wartime economy measures.

Wasserschutzpolizei (Waterways Protection Police) – responsible for policing navigable rivers and canals, regulating waterborne traffic, preventing smuggling, enforcing safety and security measures and inspecting shipping.

(b) Gendarmerie (Rural Police) – performed all Order Police functions in rural areas, and included: *Motorisierte Gendarmerie* (Motorized Traffic Gendarmerie), and *Hochgebirgs Gendarmerie* (Mountain Gendarmerie).

(c) Verwaltungspolizei (Administrative Police) – units attached to police agencies to perform the clerical and general administrative functions, to issue permits and licences and carry out subsequent inspection and regulation. These included the *Gesundheitspolizei* (Health Police), *Gewerbepolizei* (Factory & Shops Police) and *Baupolizei* (Buildings Police).

(d) Feuerschutzpolizei (Fire Protection Police) – see below under 'Fire Defence'.

(e) Luftschutzpolizei (Air Protection Police) – see below under 'Civil Defence'.

(f) Technische Nothilfe (Technical Emergency Service, TeNo) – technical auxiliary police service composed of engineers and skilled workmen, employed to perform restoration of public services both for the military and civil defence agencies in emergencies.

Supplementary to the Order Police were the *Hilfspolizei* (Auxiliary Police), consisting of unpaid civilians who performed part-time duties under supervision of the regular police: the *Landwacht* (Rural Guards) assisted the Gendarmerie, and the *Stadtwacht* (City Guards) the Schutzpolizei. In the main these Auxiliary Police were organized in collaboration with the Nazi Party; their members were lightly armed and wore a distinctive armband.

A Police Hauptwachtmeister – wearing a Wehrmacht steel helmet instead of the lighter Police model – demonstrates the correct method of moving an incendiary bomb. The local air raid precautions and response system – as opposed to the national services, run by the Air Ministry and Luftwaffe – were co-ordinated by the Order Police. In cases of major emergencies fire brigades from surrounding and even quite distant regions would be called to assist the brigades of hard-hit cities.

Sicherheitspolizei und Sicherheitsdienst der SS

The Security Police (Sipo) comprised the *Reichskriminalpolizei* (National Criminal Police, Kripo); the *Geheime Staatspolizei* (Secret State Police, Gestapo), and the *Sicherheitsdienst* (SS Security Service, SD). These organizations were all under the command of the Chef der Sicherheitspolizei und des SD – until June 1942, Reinhard Heydrich – at the head of the Reichssicherheitshauptamt (Head Office for State Security, RSHA).

Ordinary civil crimes were the concern of the Kripo, whose branch offices were usually associated closely with local units of the Schupo in cities under National Police Administration; the personnel of both worked in close co-operation in the day-to-day routine of law enforcement. The SD was the Party intelligence organization, tasked with safeguarding the Party and the Reich from subversive activity by collating information and political intelligence. Political crimes were the concern of the Gestapo, which was the executive arm of the SD; the Gestapo was not subject to any judicial or administrative control other than by its own headquarters. The *Grenzpolizei* (Frontier Police) was a uniformed branch of the Gestapo, responsible for policing the borders of Germany.

Thus it was that the Security Police and the SD formed a combination of crime specialists, political police and quasi-official political investigators, each organization maintaining its own character and fulfilling its special mission. Co-ordination was achieved through unity of command and close liaison rather than through interpenetration or control of one agency by another.

Sonderpolizei

Eleven 'Special Police' organizations were outside the normal Police structure:

Organization/controlling agency:

Eisenbahnpolizei (Railway Police)/Ministry of Transport
Bahnschutz (Railway Protection)/SS
Bergpolizei (Mines Police)/ Ministry of Economic Affairs
Forstschutzpolizei (Forestry Police)/Forestry Office
Flurschutzpolizei (Agricultural Police)/Ministry of Agriculture
Jagdpolizei (Game Conservation Police)/Forestry Office
Postschutz (Post Office Protection)/Ministry of Post & Telegraph
Zollbeamten (Customs Officials)/Ministry of Finance
Werkschutz * (Factory Protection)/Air Ministry
Deichpolizei (Dyke & Dam Police)/Ministry of Economic Affairs
Hafenpolizei (Harbour Police)/Ministry of Transport
(* Factory Protection guards were employed privately by industry, but subject to Air Ministry regulations because of their relevance to air raid precautions – see below, 'Civil Defence'.)

THE PERSECUTION OF JEWS IN GERMANY

The repressive measures inflicted upon the Jews of Germany – and subsequently those of German-occupied and fascist Europe – ranged from bureaucratic interference, through outright intimidation, confiscation, deportation and then incarceration, to final extermination. These measures grew in intensity during each successive year of the Third Reich, and the stages by which they were introduced are summarized below. Although applying specifically to Jews, their repercussions had a profound effect on the lives of many German gentiles.

In 1934 a new law made a distinction between German citizens with full political rights, including the right to vote, and second-class citizens who had no political rights. Only those Jews who could prove that their ancestors were German subjects as early as 1812 were allowed to belong to the first category (1812 was chosen because citizens assumed definite names in that year).

It was in 1935 that the most significant new restrictions were introduced. In July it was decreed that admission into the regular German Army was denied to a man if both his parents or three of his grandparents were Jewish; he could, however, be admitted to the Second Replacement Reserve. That August, Dr Josef Goebbels, Minister for Propaganda and Public Enlightenment, ordered that every Jewish musician, painter, actor, singer and writer must belong to the State

Two extremes of the executive machinery of the police state – as it wished to be seen, and as it finally revealed itself:

ABOVE LEFT **Danish volunteer factory workers seek directions from a member of the Berlin Schupo, wearing the long white coat normally used by officers on traffic duty.**

ABOVE RIGHT **The ultimate sanction of a lawless state. The final weeks before the surrender of the German forces were a time of terror – not only of the advancing Red Army and the skies full of Allied bombers, but also of fanatical last-ditch Nazis. Any sign or suspicion of weakness in the face of the enemy was enough for the 'flying (i.e. travelling) courts martial' to execute anyone, regardless of rank. Here US troops find an unfortunate Luftwaffe man, accused of attempting to desert and hanged on the orders of the SS commander in Schweinfurt.**

Association of Jewish Cultural Leagues. Jews were free to pursue their cultural activities on the explicit understanding that they desisted from playing any open part in the cultural life of the German people. The following month, non-Aryan dealers in arts and antiquities were given notice to liquidate their businesses within four weeks. In 1935 Jews owned about 80 per cent of such firms in Germany; this enforced liquidation caused the market to become overstocked, with a consequent sharp drop in prices.

Also in September, Minister of Education Bernhard Rust decreed the establishment of special elementary schools for Jewish children as from 1 April 1936; the teachers were to be Jews, selected from those who had been placed on pension since the Nazis came to power. Children who had one or both Jewish parents were sent to these schools, but those whose Jewish blood came only from grandparents were allowed to attend ordinary schools.

The 1935 annual Nazi Party Congress held at Nuremberg in September was used to announce further anti-Jewish laws. The first of these limited full citizenship to people of pure German blood, and made the distinction between the 'state citizen' (Reichsbürger) and the 'state subject', the latter to be identified by a special identity document; only Reich citizens were to enjoy full civil and political rights. The second new law forbade marriage or sexual relations between Jews and Germans or other 'Aryans'.

In October 1935 the first series of executive regulations for the application of these measures was issued. By the Nazi definition, a 'full Jew' – who belonged to the Jewish faith or who had at least three Jewish grandparents – could not become a Reich citizen, nor could they hold any official post. 'Partial Jews' were those having no more than two Jewish grandparents. If they did not belong to the Jewish faith and were not married to a Jew, these were permitted to become Reich citizens, although the Minister of the Interior could revoke this privilege. Under the Nazi law 'for the Protection of German Blood and Honour' no Jew was allowed to marry a German. 'Half Jews' (persons with two Jewish grandparents) wishing to marry Germans had to apply to the Ministry of the Interior, who made enquiries into the supplicant's family history, character, and physical and moral qualities. Marriages between 'quarter Jews' were absolutely forbidden (so as not to perpetuate the Jewish strain in their blood), but they were free to marry Aryans.

That same month the Propaganda Ministry forbade the inscription of the names of fallen Jews on monuments to the German war dead; however, there was no order to obliterate Jewish names from existing memorials.

On 21 November 1935 the Minister of Economic Affairs, Dr Schacht, ordered that all Jewish stockbrokers on German exchanges were to give up their offices immediately (this was considered a public office). A few days later the Ministry of Propaganda forbade Jewish artists, writers, actors and singers from using pseudonyms, to prevent them passing themselves off as Aryans; by law, Jewish artists could only appear before Jewish audiences.

In February 1936 Dr Gerhard Wagner, national leader of the German medical profession, decreed the creation of a list of Jewish doctors in Germany, prohibited the future admission of Jews to the profession, and regulated the relations between Jewish and non-Jewish doctors; Jews were

also barred from the veterinary profession. Two months later it was announced that persons wishing to work in journalism or publishing had to provide the Press Control Board with documentary proof of pure German or racially related blood of both husband and wife back to the year 1800 (instead of to the grandparents, as formerly).

Not surprisingly, three years of relentless persecution had its effect on the Jewish population of Germany, which dropped from 499,682 to 409,000 between June 1933 and April 1936.

In November 1936, at Munich University, Professor Walter Frank, head of the Institute for Historical Studies of the New Germany, addressed over 300 professors representing the country's leading universities and technical schools, on the opening of the National Socialist Institute for Research into the History of the Jews and Study of Jewish Questions. Munich was chosen for the establishment of a new anti-Jewish library, housing the largest collection of books on the subject in Europe.

By the beginning of 1938 anti-Semitic measures were far surpassing the 1935 Nuremberg Laws. In December 1937 Jewish doctors who had fought in the Great War, and had thus retained their practices, were notified that patients belonging to certain National Health Insurance categories were no longer allowed to consult them. Many Jews and half-Jews were having their passports confiscated or not renewed on expiry; permission to leave Germany was only being given either for permanent emigration, or for business trips of profit to the state. Both Jewish directors and workers, whenever possible, were driven from the clothing industry – once largely controlled by that community – and a new employers' union pledged to have no dealings with Jewish contractors, wholesalers or retailers. Jews were also excluded from the auction business.

Crude and violent 'Jew-baiting' on an extensive scale was commonplace in Berlin and some other cities. Practically all Jewish shops, and doctors' and dentists' premises, were placarded or daubed with offensive inscriptions identifying the owners as non-Aryan; the

Police did not interfere with this. In June 1938 an amendment to the Nuremberg Laws defined what was a 'Jewish undertaking', decreeing the registration of all such businesses, and the identification of their premises by a yellow disc on a square or rectangular black background. By 20 July most of the shops in the west of Berlin – those largely visited by tourists and foreigners – were permitted to remove the daubed window inscriptions and to reopen; in the east of the city, however, where the poorer Jews congregated, the graffiti remained untouched and nearly every Jewish business remained closed. A decree of 3 August 1938 cancelled, as from 30 September, the diplomas of all Jewish medical practitioners in Germany.

A further decree on 11 August, by Minister of the Interior Dr Frick and Minister of Justice Dr Gürtner, instructed that in future Jews were allowed to give only such personal names to their children as were approved by the Ministry of the Interior as 'typically Jewish'; moreover, as from 1 January 1939, every male Jewish subject of the Reich had to add the name 'Israel' to that which he already bore, while females had to take the name 'Sarah'. (Lists of approved names were issued; these included many unusual biblical names completely unknown to the German Jewish community, but excluded several which were also popular among German Christians – e.g. Josef, Jakob, Ruth and Esther.) These additional names had to be used in all official and business transactions, and reported to the local registrar who had recorded their births and marriages (or, if they lived abroad, to the local German consul). Contraventions were, as always, punishable with imprisonment and fines.

A further decree from the Ministry of the Interior on 7 October 1938 invalidated all passports held by Jews living in Germany and ordered them to surrender their passports within 14 days. Since 1933 some 150,000 German Jews had fled the country, many of them having to abandon almost everything they owned; the remainder would now face enormous difficulties in trying to emigrate. However, an estimated 20,000 Polish Jews residing in the Reich were arrested and actually transported in special trains direct to the German–Polish border. Of these about 8,000 were forced across the frontier before, by agreement with the Polish government, the German authorities suspended the expulsions (after several hundred Germans had been arrested in Poland as a reprisal).

On 7 November 1938, Ernst von Rath, Third Secretary of the German Embassy in Paris, was shot by Herschel Grynszpan, a 17-year-old Polish Jew whose aged parents were among those deported and now suffering privations while held at the frontier. Von Rath died from his wounds two days later, and this led to an outbreak of anti-Jewish violence throughout Germany and Austria on 9–10 November, in what were described by the London *Times* as 'scenes of systematic plunder and destruction which have seldom had their equal in a civilised country, since the time of the Middle Ages'. All over the Reich synagogues were set on fire or dynamited, Jewish shops and homes were smashed and ransacked, and individual Jews arrested or hunted through the streets by bands of young Nazis. Large crowds participated, but Police interference was confined to taking the owners of Jewish premises into 'protective custody'. In Berlin alone, 8,000 Jews were arrested during this so-called 'Krystallnacht' ('Night of the Broken Glass'). The fire brigades remained similarly inactive, merely protecting neighbouring houses from any spreading of the flames. The foreign press reported that the 'spontaneous' outrages – which were in fact carefully planned and carried out simultaneously in all parts of the Reich – were regarded with shame and disgust by large sections of the German people.

On the evening of 10 November, Goebbels proclaimed that the 'demonstrations' stemming from the 'justified and understandable indignation of the German people' must cease – but two days later he used the event to announce punitive measures against not the rioters, but the Jews. As from 1 January 1939 Jews were forbidden to own retail shops, mail-order firms or export businesses, or to engage in independent handicrafts; no Jew was to be a manager of any concern, and Jews occupying leading positions without managerial status could be dismissed at six weeks' notice. The damage done to Jewish property had to be made good by the Jews themselves; insurance claims by Jews of German nationality were confiscated by the Reich, and the Jewish population was forced to pay the Reich a collective fine of 1,000 million marks (the equivalent in 1939 of £83 million, and of perhaps 30 times that amount today). The persecution of German Jews, pursued with the utmost vigour, was rapidly reducing them to a proletarian community dependent on charity. Despite the obstacles placed in their way, some 100,000 more Jews managed to leave Germany between Krystallnacht and September 1939.

After the outbreak of war the situation for the perhaps 250,000 remaining Jews in Germany became utterly isolated and helpless. On 7 August 1940 it was announced that all Germans had to furnish themselves with an Ahnenpass (Certificate of Ancestry), a 50-page booklet proving their 'racial purity' back to at least the year 1800 (hitherto such documents had only been required for members of the Party, the SA and SS). A new wave of terror began on 6 September 1941 when a decree by Reinhard Heydrich, Himmler's deputy as head of the RSHA, compelled all Jews over the age of six to wear a prominent yellow Star of David badge bearing the inscription 'Jude' in characters resembling Hebrew, on their coats, jackets or dresses when appearing in public, and at the same time forbade them to leave their places of residence without written police permission.

The German invasion of Poland in September 1939 had been followed by the first mass murders of Jews in the occupied territories; these accelerated enormously with the invasion of the USSR in June 1941, and from that stage onwards the history of German persecution of the Jews belongs to that of the 'Final Solution', which has no place here.

SS General Reinhard Heydrich (1904–42), Himmler's formidable deputy; a notably vain man, he is photographed here in fencing costume. It was allegedly a sexual scandal that obliged him, in 1931, to resign his commission in the Navy, where he had been an intelligence officer serving under the future Admiral Canaris. Heydrich founded the SD in Munich that same year, and rose quickly through the Nazi hierarchy by a combination of ruthless ambition, conspiracy, threats and blackmail. He was chief of the Sipo from 1934, and of Head Office for State Security from 1939. Always rumoured to have Jewish blood himself, he was a violent anti-Semite, and in January 1942 he presided over the Wannsee conference that revealed to other ministries the true nature of the 'Final Solution'. (Topham Picturepoint)

EMPLOYMENT

The State Labour Service

Since the 1920s many voluntary work camps had been established by youth, church and political orgnizations and local authorities, providing both labour for public works and employment for those without it; these became a national organization in 1931. Named the State Labour Service (Reichsarbeitsdienst, RAD) in July 1934, this was later divided into the male RAD/Männer and the female RAD/weibliche Jugend ('for young women').

From June 1935 all non-Jewish men had to complete six months' RAD/M service between the ages of 18 and 25, before their compulsory two years' military service (which was reintroduced in May 1935); volunteers could do a full year's RAD service. They received pre-military and physical training; their work was largely agricultural, but included land drainage and development of wasteland and waterways. Organization was quasi-military, in divisional districts (Arbeitsgaue), regiments, battalions and companies; cadres were provided by officers and NCOs who had completed their military service. When general mobilization was decreed in August 1939 the RAD/M had 360,000 members, more than half of whom were transferred to the Wehrmacht Bautruppen (Construction Troops). After the Polish campaign the RAD/M was rebuilt on its pre-war basis, and during wartime it supported Wehrmacht engineers in work on all kinds of infrastructure projects.

In August 1936 the Ministry of the Interior announced the imminent introduction of six months' compulsory service in the RAD for young women. Some RAD/wJ camps were established in agricultural districts where the girls helped farming families; others, in districts of new settlement, where they made themselves generally useful to the settlers; and still others, in distressed industrial areas, where the girls did the housework and cared for the children of working women. Generally, conditions of service for the female RAD were a good deal less stern and regimented than for young men; the regime reassured families that their daughters' physical and moral welfare would be carefully protected.

The six-month period of pre-military service spent in the National Labour Service (RAD) was supposed to toughen young men up physically and instill a sense of group discipline, while performing useful public works. Swamps were drained, canals and irrigation ditches repaired (as here), ground cleared and roads built.

A further decree of 29 July 1941 established a young women's Auxiliary War Service scheme, for work in government offices, nursing, social work and domestic help to large families, for a duration of six months following their original six months' RAD/wJ service. (This was independent of the 'obligatory year' for girls leaving school who later wished to enter factories, and had first to work for a year as a household help; a 'farm year' had also been instituted by the Hitler Youth for the 'strengthening of the bonds between the urban and rural areas'.)

It was not until after December 1941 that RAD/wJ girls could be deployed to armaments and munitions factories or to the female auxiliary services of the Wehrmacht (see Plate Commentaries, F1 & H2). Despite resistance from the Oberkommando der Wehrmacht, the need for women in military support roles became irresistible, and by the end of the war some 80,000 RAD/wJ 'Work-Maidens' were employed in various roles in the air defence system and perhaps 20,000 more on other roles for the armed forces. These were in addition to the 470,000-odd members of the formal, uniformed military auxiliary organizations.

A works foreman checks some paperwork with a young apprentice; note, centre and right background, men in the dark blue uniform of the DAF (see Plate D1). From the first, Germany's economy was completely inadequate to sustain a long war. Hitler's decision to invade the USSR in 1941 was an act of economic madness, apparently based on the delusion that plundering new occupied territories could provide the necessary resources.

Directed state employment

When the Four-Year Plan was announced at the Party Congress of 1936, there existed a reserve of about one million unemployed. By the end of May 1938 the able-bodied unemployed had dwindled to only 37,000, and the number of employed persons had risen from about 12 million at the beginning of 1933 to 20.5 million. Thus there were hardly any reserves of male labour to draw upon for the execution of work that was judged to be urgent in the interests of the state.

A period of compulsory employment for all German men and some women (who enjoyed many exemptions) was instituted by a decree of 22 June 1938 issued by Göring as Commissioner of the Four-Year Plan. The decree, which took effect from 1 July, stated that every able-bodied man and woman was obliged to perform work in a specific post allotted for a limited period of time, or to prepare for a particular profession. Drafted men and women would earn no less than they had hitherto, and they retained the right to return to their previous posts when their terms of state employment were completed. Persons deemed fit for a special type of job could be drafted from any profession or trade, but labour was to be conscripted in this way only for production work of national importance. The decision as to which undertakings qualified rested with the Commissioner for the Four-Year Plan.

Wartime mobilization

The shortage of labour caused by military conscription led to concerns in the essential industries and agriculture, and greatly reduced the

The origins of this welder are identified by the blue-and-white 'Ost' (East) patch sewn to his jacket. German industry came to rely heavily on workers from the occupied territories; by October 1942 these totalled 3.5 million, and that figure would double over the following 18 months. Initially many were volunteers from Western countries, although these soon discovered that their conditions were much worse than advertised; the bulk of them, however, were forced labourers from Poland and further east. This influx was unpopular with the German urban public, though farmers were too glad of the extra hands to worry much about the risk of crime from their Polish and French labourers. The foreigners were most popular of all with industry, since their pay and conditions of work were far less burdensome than when employing Germans – especially, German women. The treatment of Eastern workers was extremely harsh; in February 1943, Goebbels argued that for pragmatic reasons it should be liberalized, but he was resisted by the SS.

supply of consumer goods and services; for instance, by June 1940 employment in the leather, textiles, clothing and woodworking industries had already fallen by 50 per cent. The demand for labour became increasingly critical, particularly when the scope of military conscription was widened following the German failure before Moscow in December 1941 and again after the disaster at Stalingrad a year later. Incentives were used, as well as compulsion; the Nazis made 'pie in the sky' promises of a generous new old age pension scheme, and large-scale provision of social housing – but only after final victory.

The major method used to meet the shortfall was the employment and conscription of foreign workers and prisoners of war from the occupied countries. In May 1939 the total labour force counted 39.1 million Germans and only 300,000 foreigners; in May 1944 the figures were just under 29 million Germans and 7.1 million foreigners, the latter total made up of 1.8 million prisoners of war and 5.3 million civilians.

A decree at the end of April 1942 declared that 'economic necessities are more important than schooling', and provided for compulsory labour until that November by children above the age of ten, from both urban and rural areas, in farm camps run by the Hitler Youth.

Drastic steps were also taken to increase the adult German labour force, especially of skilled workers. In July 1942 a decree forbade employers from offering high wages to poach skilled hands, and workers were forbidden from moving jobs without permission. In fact labour discipline was generally good among the age-groups who might otherwise find themselves called up for the Russian Front (immunities on grounds of age and family responsibility were progressively removed); it was less so among women and teenage boys.

At the time of Stalingrad, when Eastern Front casualties were running at about 150,000 per month and monthly reinforcements at a maximum of 65,000, the adoption of a 'Total War' economy was announced to free more men for military service. On 27 January 1943 all men aged 16 to 65 were ordered to register with their local labour offices. On 30 January, all non-essential trades and commercial businesses were given notice to close down, the released manpower to register for, e.g., factory work. Goebbels was always tempted to attack the wealthy classes, and specifically included in his decree some of Berlin's finest restaurants; such gestures infuriated Göring, who defiantly frustrated them. More damagingly, many thousands of small businesses, shops and cafés closed (the Gauleiter of Mark Brandenburg reported that by 9 May more than 9,000 firms had closed in his Gau alone). This measure was so unpopular with the petit-bourgeois social class, among whom the Nazis had always enjoyed their warmest support, that it was rescinded that September.

By 1944 bombing was seriously affecting the economy, and on 1 August a decree introduced a total ban on vacations, and a compulsory 60-hour week in all factories and offices without payment for overtime. From then on the plight of workers and their families became increasingly unbearable. They had to travel to work and back by constantly disrupted public transport. Families might have been evacuated far away, or be living in crowded accommodation with relatives and friends, or billeted on resentful strangers. After long working days, and fulfilling compulsory air-raid precaution duty, their sleep was repeatedly interrupted by the need to go to the shelters. Those who lived in cities or industrial areas went in daily fear for their lives; and all the time supplies of food and every other necessity of life were desperately short and unreliable.

Women in the labour force

German women played important roles in sustaining health and welfare, transport, the civil service and – eventually – industry; but Hitler and

BOTTOM LEFT **Young women of the RAD/wJ, and younger girls of the Bund Deutsche Mädel (the female equivalent of the Hitler Jugend – see Plate F2), were encouraged to work on the land and in industry. The brooches worn at their throats identify these two as RAD/wJ 'Work-Maidens'.**

BOTTOM RIGHT **A young woman undertaking essential factory work. Pinned to her tie is the RAD** *Kriegshilfsdienstabzeichen*, **the 'War Auxiliary Service Badge' established in July 1941 for those RAD girls who had completed an extra six months' service in support of the war effort after finishing their obligatory first six months. Women's wages were generally 75–80 per cent those paid to men, although a few categories – e.g. drivers – could qualify for equal pay.**

23

other leading Nazis held deeply conservative views about conscripting women into the labour force. In their eyes the proper contribution of women was bearing and raising children and caring for homes. They were nervous about changes to gender roles in German society, and about alienating servicemen by conscripting their wives. They held strong prejudices about 'suitable' work for women, and even in the most educated professions women faced a rigid 'glass ceiling' which took little account of their true abilities.

By 1942 some 52 per cent of the German labour force were women, in at least part-time jobs, but the absolute numbers hardly changed throughout the war. In May 1940 they numbered about 14.6 million, of which the greatest number (some 6.5 million) worked in agriculture. In May 1944 the total was still only 14.8 million women, of whom agriculture accounted for about 5.7 million (this being a field to which many foreign labourers had been directed). Throughout the war, German leaders were much more hesitant and contradictory than the British about getting women into industry. In Britain, from spring 1941, all women aged 18 to 50 who were single or married without dependants had to register for employment; many mothers also campaigned successfully for government child-care arrangements so that they could voluntarily take paid work. In December 1941 the British government was empowered to conscript all single and women and childless widows aged 19 to 30, who if actually called up, were given the options of joining the women's auxiliary branches of the armed forces or doing factory or agricultural work, often in areas distant from their homes.

In Germany, between September 1939 and May 1940 the proportion of working women actually dropped, since family allowances for wives of military conscripts made it more attractive to stay at home. In March 1941 Gauleiters were told to encourage women to take voluntary jobs, but conscription was not allowed. Family allowances were altered that June to encourage childless wives to register for work. The crisis of December 1941 brought Gauleiter Fritz Sauckel of Thüringia the post of State Plenipotentiary for Labour Mobilization; although an enthusiast for female conscription, who tinkered with the system to bring in more women, Sauckel was still thwarted by Hitler and some other senior Nazis.

The system always made a distinction between those who had been in work before September 1939 – who were subject to gradually increasing pressures – and those who had not. In other words, the working classes were much more likely to be put in factories than the middle classes; and class resentment against the 'idle, shirking wealthy' ran deep and bitter in all Party and SD reports on public morale throughout the war. In April 1942 Sauckel argued with Göring to be

A young woman volunteer helping with the after-effects of an air raid queues up for a meal from a public soup kitchen. She wears work trousers, like many women, and this practical habit led to a dilemma for conservative Nazi authorities, who were always woried about the changes in gender roles forced upon the population by wartime necessity. Accustomed to trousers for work, many women aroused protests when they took to wearing smarter versions in the street; in Gau Württemberg-Hohenzollern this was actually banned by law. The SS were more relaxed about such trivia, and in December 1944 Himmler ordered the Police not to prosecute.

allowed to share out the burdens of war more equally among German women; Göring replied with crashing snobbery that 'A thoroughbred harnessed to the plough becomes exhausted quicker than a workhorse. The main task for women of good breeding is having children.'

After Stalingrad the demands of 'total war' made pressure for conscription irresistible, and Hitler was nagged into allowing Sauckel to decree on 27 January 1943 that all women aged 17 to 45 must register for work (exempting the pregnant, mothers with children under school age or two children under 14, and certain other categories). The wealthier classes still managed to manipulate the system to obtain exemptions; and in fact, employers were reluctant to take on (or to keep for long) women workers, who were less skilled than foreigners and more costly to employ. Only in July 1944 did Hitler finally allow the extension of compulsory labour registration to women aged 45–50.

CIVIL LIFE

Public health

Each Stadtkreis, Landkreis and Gemeinde had an Office for Public Health (Gesundheitsamt), under a medical director (Amtsarzt) who was a permanently employed state official. Although his activities were strictly controlled by superior officials, he had considerable local power in the exercise of his duties. The Amtsarzt was the supervisor of all practising physicians, dentists, midwives, pharmacists and even veterinarians within his district, and the official spokesman of the local medical organizations. He was responsible for the education, training and distribution of all auxiliary medical personnel not employed in public institutions. As local head of the Health Police he inspected the conditions of dwellings, industrial plants and public buildings, as well as hospitals and institutions. He was responsible for water purification, sewage and garbage disposal, air and soil hygiene, and the local burial system. He supervised all local food and dairy plants and stores. He prepared weekly reports and statistics on communicable diseases and other subjects; he personally supervised the control of epidemics in his locality, and arranged for the immunization of children and adults. The Amtsarzt ensured that all persons with venereal disease or tuberculosis underwent proper treatment; he supervised the trade in drugs, patent medicines and poisons; he co-ordinated

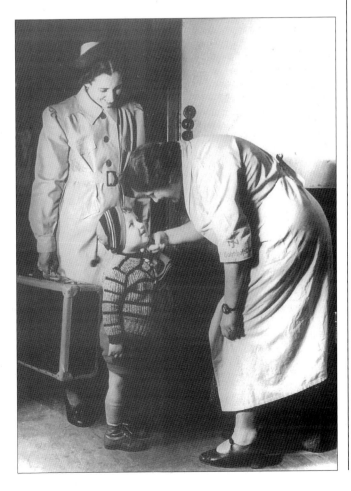

Identified by her armband as being on duty at a railway station, this nursing auxiliary in the NS-Schwesternschaft takes an interest in a young lad and his mother. These sisters were Party members contributing their time and work to the NS-Volkswohl-fahrt (National Socialist Welfare Organization).

Interior view of a German Red Cross rapid response vehicle, looking from the front towards the rear doors. In addition to the crew this large bus, with convertible seats and removable stretchers, was capable of carrying 18 stretcher cases or 30 seated patients.

with voluntary health organizations maintained by the Nazi Party, the German Red Cross and the churches, and supervised the athletic programmes of the various youth organizations. As the local Police doctor, he performed autopsies in all medico-legal cases, gave testimony in court, and issued health certificates. To fulfil these duties, the Amtsarzt of a heavily populated district had a staff of auxiliary physicians, sanitary inspectors, veterinarians and junior medical personnel, and remote areas had additional branch offices.

One of the most important Nazi laws made the Amtsarzt in effect the 'Protector of German Blood and Honour' within his locality; he advised on marriages, issued the health and race certificates necessary for obtaining marriage licences, and directed propaganda to encourage a higher birthrate. He represented the Reich agency for maternal and child welfare, granted marriage loans, and initiated the steps leading to the termination of undesirable pregnancies. The Amsarzt also initiated the sterilization of the insane, alcoholics, sex criminals, and persons with hereditary physical defects, and was responsible for the admission of the mentally and physically disabled and chronic invalids to public institutions. Between October 1939 and August 1941 a euthanasia programme for 'incurables' – ordered by Hitler himself in a hand-written note to the head of his Chancellery, Philip Bouhler – saw the murder by physicians of more than 70,000 mentally ill Germans. Although SS medical officers were involved, this was not primarily an SS but a Party project, carried out largely by civilian medical staff. Its lessons were studied during the planning of the 'Final Solution'.

RATIONING & SHORTAGES
Food

Despite the wholesale plunder of harvests and livestock from newly conquered and occupied countries, the availability and distribution of food and clothing throughout Germany became progressively worse throughout the whole war. Although official food prices in Germany did not rise more than 10 per cent, this did not, of course, apply to the prices charged by black-marketeers. (By the second half of the war bartering for goods and services was widespread; civilians did not regard this as a crime as long as it was done on behalf of individual families, but they supported drastic punishments for large-scale black-marketeering for profit.)

Lack of manpower had a serious effect on German agriculture, which was only overcome by the use of youth labour, prisoners of war and foreign labourers. The regime made a conscious and successful effort to improve over the rationing system which had caused such unrest during World War I. Consumers were divided into 'groups' by their type of work or domestic status. The basic calculation was that rations for 'normal consumers' (roughly 40 per cent of the total population) were to be based on 2,400 calories per day; for 'heavy workers', on 3,600 calories; and for 'very heavy workers', on 4,200 calories. There were special arrangements for children in various groups, adolescents, and self-suppliers (i.e. farmers). In November 1939 intermediate scales were introduced for those working long-shifts (ten hours or more) in any category, and for night shift workers. Naturally, there was much dispute among those who considered that

A member of an SA squad helping after an air raid sits on a coiled fire hose while he receives first aid; he seems to have suffered both head injuries and burns to his hands. After Hitler's bloody purge of the SA leadership on 30 June 1934 the Stormtroopers were replaced by the vastly enlarged SS as the main instrument of Nazi power over the population, but as a nationwide, voluntary, part-time organization they remained useful. Members performed many general duties requiring a mass of representatives throughout the country (e.g., making public collections, distributing public information leaflets, etc), and also provided physical and pre-military training.

they had been wrongly categorized. There is no space here for more than a summary of the situation in 1939 and one or two important later alterations to the rationing scheme.

On 27 August 1939 rationing was introduced for the civilian population. Initially most foodstuffs were rationed, together with clothing, shoes, leather and soap. An official statement explained that the introduction of rationing had been decided upon 'to equip us for a war of any possible duration... Ration cards are not an acute emergency measure, but only the precaution of a responsible government that has learned its lesson from the blunders of the Great War.' By 25 September 1939 the distribution of ration cards throughout the Reich had been completed.

For the purpose of food rationing, Germany was divided into 32 agricultural regions, the main planning for which was carried out at Land or Provinz level; under these regional offices were 710 county (Kreis) and about 60,000 local offices of the National Food Estate. At regional, county and local levels this agency was divided into two departments: Abteilung A, concerned with agricultural production, food processing, the inspection of farms and their compulsory records; and Abteilung B, which dealt with the consumer – ration cards, definition of consumer categories, lists of households, and the distribution of food from wholesalers.

Practically every type of foodstuff was rationed, either on a national basis or by a system of local distribution. Foods rationed nationally were: bread, Nährmittel (cereal products, alimentary pastes, potato-flour, etc), meats, fats, cheese, sugar, jam, coffee substitutes, cocoa, artificial honey and whole milk. Cocoa and artificial honey were reserved for children, and whole milk for children, expectant and nursing mothers, invalids and for workers in certain unhealthy occupations (e.g. the lead and aluminium industries). Bread and flour had not been included initially but were rapidly added to the list, the generous normal weekly allowance being 85oz (5.3lb) per person, including 13.5oz of flour.

Unlike Britain, there was no 'points' system for food rationing in Germany. The following list gives the national allowances of some main items per head per week (converted into British weights and measures) for 'normal consumers' under the revised scales of 25 September 1939:

Meat	20oz
Fats	12oz
Sugar	9oz
Jam	3.5oz
Bread & flour	85oz – reduced in July 1940 by 5.3oz for all adults.

Men doing 'heavy' or 'very heavy' manual work were entitled to an extra allowance of bread and meat, which could be as much as double the normal ration. 'Fat cards' secured a butter ration of 3oz, while the cheese ration was slightly over 2oz weekly. Most adults could buy only skimmed milk. The ration for substitute (Ersatz) tea was fixed at 0.75oz and for substitute coffee at 2oz per week, real tea and coffee having disappeared from the market with the cutting of sea lanes. A special card secured a series of articles such as eggs (averaging about 4 per month), artificial honey, dried vegetables and cocoa if and when these were available.

In 1939 foods that could be obtained without national ration cards included potatoes, fresh fruit, vegetables, fish, onions and skimmed milk; however, due to the great regional variations in German transport conditions and other factors, these commodities were often rationed on a local basis by means of 'control cards'.

Ration cards (actually, sheets of paper) covered periods of 28 days; they were variously coloured (e.g., red for bread coupons), and were obtained from local food offices or card offices (Kartenstellen) set up in villages and larger towns. Separate cards of distinctive colours were issued for certain commodities, and supplementary cards for long-hours and night workers and those undertaking heavy work were issued by employers – this encouraged stability among valuable employees. There were also 'leave cards' and 'travel stamps', which were issued in lieu of the normal ration cards to the relevant groups.

No rationed foodstuffs could be obtained in shops, restaurants, factories or catering establishments without the surrender of coupons. Retailers received from their customers order vouchers (Bestellscheine), food cards and leave card coupons, and any special vouchers or coupons issued for e.g. the sick. Restaurateurs received from their clients food and leave card coupons and travel stamps. They exchanged these at the food office for Bezugsscheine (buying permits), which enabled them to purchase from wholesalers; the latter, in turn, exchanged the Bezugsscheine for Grossbezugesscheine, which enabled them to purchase in bulk from manufacturers, distributors or producers.

Restaurants and hotels were originally allowed to sell dishes without ration cards on condition that they had two meatless days per week and a restricted menu; after this led to a run on restaurants, the exemption was removed from 2 October 1939. As from 1 January 1942 the flesh of dogs, foxes, bears and beavers became legal articles of diet; and from 12 January, all German restaurants were ordered to serve a 'field-kitchen' dish (for which not more than 17.6oz of meat and 3.5oz of general food or bread could be used) on Mondays and Thursdays, with Tuesdays and Fridays remaining meatless days.

Weekly ration cards were issued for foreign civilian workers who were gainfully employed but not working on farms, fed in canteens or accommodated in camps. The cards were issued through the establishments employing them, and these handed in the used cards to their appropriate food office complete with lists of the names. Those accommodated in camps were placed on the basic scale for long-hours and night workers, and the appropriate supplements for heavy work were added.

Writing in '*Das Reich*' on 29 March 1942, Goebbels announced a new decree against hoarders and black-marketeers, declaring that 'whoever destroys, hides or withholds raw materials or products [and] thereby deliberately endangers public supplies' would be punished by imprisonment, penal servitude or, in severe cases, by death.

The cuts of 1942

As from 6 April 1942 the weekly bread, meat and fat rations were all reduced. Of the new bread ration, only one-fifth was available as white bread or flour, with the balance in rye or inferior mixed-grain bread; and at the same time national rationing was introduced even for potatoes. In 1940/41 the proportion of non-rationed foodstuffs in the average household diet was more than 20 per cent; by the end of 1942 it was only 0.3 per cent. The cuts were explained as being due to poor harvests resulting from bad weather; lack of agricultural labour; greatly increased requirements from the armed forces; increases in the rations needed for heavy and night workers by one million since the first year of the war; the presence of millions of foreign workers, prisoners of war and repatriated ethnic Germans (Volksdeutsche); and the need to send food supplies to other friendly countries. It was admitted that in spite of all pre-war preparations the food situation had deteriorated slowly but steadily since 1939, and that there were no immediate prospects of using captured cornfields in the Ukraine to relieve the position. The cuts in rations had a seriously depressing effect on the civilian population; women became ever more worried about feeding their families, and workers protested that the rations were not enough to sustain them during long shifts and disrupted journeys.

Consumer goods

The rationing of consumer goods was the function of the Ministry of Economic Affairs. Clothing, textiles and footwear were rationed by a point system; each consumer was given a clothing card with a value of a specified number of points. The cost in points of each item of clothing was listed, and consumers were allowed to spend their points as they saw fit. The methods whereby other consumer goods were rationed varied considerably, and included combinations of points, special permits, absolute limitations, propaganda appeals, sliding scales and outright prohibitions. Numerous differences based upon type of work, age, and physical status applied to clothing rations and the permits for other household consumer goods.

Shortages of practically everything gradually increased as the war progressed, greatly aggravated by the air raids from spring 1942 onwards.

Homes were destroyed, their contents burnt, smashed or inextricably buried. Survivors had little time or opportunity to salvage household goods, and replacement of such losses proved either difficult or impossible after producers and retailers were closed down or diverted to war work.

Compulsory collections

A report by the US Board of Economic Warfare published on 28 April 1943 estimated that by the end of 1941 looting by the Germans throughout occupied Europe had already amounted to a value of at least £9 billion (in 1941 values, £9,000 million, or US$36 billion; in today's values, about 30 times as much), and that the rate had since accelerated to tens of billions of dollars annually. This plunder included every type of military hardware, industrial plant, railway stock (even tracks), manufactured goods, foodstuffs of every kind and livestock.

Although enough steel scrap had been taken from France alone to cover normal German exports for three and a half years, the drive to collect more within the Reich was intensified. In March 1940 all bronze bells were requisitioned. On 26 March 1941 an intensive campaign for the collection of all scrap metal (including iron railings, etc) was inaugurated by Göring; the death penalty was threatened for anybody withholding metal or profiting from trading in it, the last date for the surrender of metal by households being fixed for 20 April 1941 (Hitler's birthday).

A month later all copper and aluminium coins began to be withdrawn from circulation and replaced by zinc coins.

The salvaging from damaged homes of anything retrievable was an essential post-raid service. Recovered and still usable furniture was usually removed when transport became available, and stored by the Self-Protection Service and local Party in warehouses in a 'safe area', to be either reclaimed by the owners or offered to other bombed-out families who were being re-housed.

PROPAGANDA & CENSORSHIP

The manipulation of opinion, by the dissemination of the official 'line' and the limiting of all other sources of information, was considered to be of the utmost importance, and state control was almost watertight. State propaganda was spread via the radio, the national press, and the film and theatre industry. Censorship was imposed in order to limit what the populace saw, read and heard to what the Party wanted them to know.

National and provincial newspapers had flourished in pre-Nazi Germany, but National Socialism put many of them out of business. As early as July 1931 the pre-Nazi government had published an Emergency Order under which editors would be obliged, if requested by government authorities, to publish – free, and without addition or omission – information from government sources, together with refutations of facts previously stated in the publication concerned. In February 1933 the Communist and Socialist press in Prussia was 'temporarily' suppressed in the aftermath of the burning of the Reichstag. The Minister of the Interior was also empowered to stop the circulation in Germany of foreign publications that broke the rules laid down for the home press – among the hardest of these to avoid was the circulation of 'obviously false news through which the vital interest of the state may be endangered'.

In June 1933, 254 foreign newspapers and periodicals were banned from Germany; unlike the German press, they did not have a legal right to appeal against suspension. On 29 December 1939 a further ban was introduced on the entry into the Reich of all papers and journals published abroad in the German language.

(An incidental decision was announced on 1 June 1941, when the traditional Gothic-style printer's typeface was officially abandoned in German newspapers, and lettering in Roman type substituted; the reason given was that the New Order in Europe made it necessary for foreigners be able to read German with ease. The substitution of Roman for Gothic handwriting was later made obligatory in all schools.)

Radio broadcasting

The production of a new People's Radio Set complete with mains connection and loudspeakers was announced to coincide with the German Radio Exhibition that opened in Berlin on 5 August 1938. Over 700,000 sets were manufactured that year, and offered for sale at 35 marks each.

The State Broadcasting Service, headed by Dr Heinrich Glasmeier, came under a department of the Propaganda Ministry. Control of the broadcasting available to the public was considered vitally important; in September 1939 a decree threatened dire penalties for listening to the BBC and other foreign stations, and for repeating what was heard from them. At first Dr Goebbels even drafted an order for the mass confiscation of all civilian radio sets, but he was quickly talked out of this panicky move. Prosecutions for listening to foreign stations were the responsibility of the Gestapo, and long sentences of imprisonment and hard labour were handed out by the Special Courts. By July 1940 nearly 2,200 arrests had already been made; of these 1,171 resulted in legal proceedings, 118 people were acquitted, and 708 imprisoned.

(continued on page 41)

1: *SA-Gruppenführer, 1939–43*
2: *NSDAP-Dienstleiter*
3: Fireman, Berlin *Feuerschutzpolizei*

A

1: Fireman, *Sicherheits u.Hilfsdienst*, winter 1941/42
2: *LSW-Oberzugführer, Luftschutzwarndienst*
3: *Hauptluftschutz-Führer, Reichsluftschutzbund*

B

1: *OT-Kameradschaftsführer, Organisation Todt, 1942–43*
2: *Vormann, Reichsarbeitsdienst*
3: *TN-Vormann, Technische Nothilfe, 1941–42*

C

1: Female postal worker, *Deutsche Reichspost*
2: DRB railway conductress, 1941–42
3: *DRK-Anwärter, Deutsche Rote Kreuz*

E

1: *Luftwaffe Flakwaffenhelferin*, winter 1943/44
2: *BD-Mädchen, Bund Deutsche Mädel*, winter 1939/40
3: *HJ-Oberkameradschaftsführer, Luftwaffenhelfer-Hitler Jugend*

F

1: *Bzp-Unterzugführer, Bahnschutzpolizei,* c.1942
2: *Oberwachtmeister, Schutzpolizei des Reiches,* c.1942
3: National staff member, *NS-Frauenschaft*

1: *Volkssturmmann*, 1945
2: *Nachrichtenhelferin, Nachrichten Dienst des Heeres*
3: *HJ-Rottenführer, HJ-Streifendienst, 1944–45*

H

Goebbels took a close personal interest in programming, and he understood that to keep their audience a good proportion of broadcasts had to be entertaining; he warned that an unrelieved diet of heavy patriotic material would cause listeners, including servicemen, to tune to the BBC simply to hear the light music they enjoyed. However, although Goebbels has often been described as a propaganda genius, he failed – before at least January 1943 – to curb broadcasts in terms of exaggerated contempt for Allied leaders and troops, and the bombastic trumpeting of German successes. The public soon learned to distrust these, due to information from front-line personnel and the evidence of their own growing hardships. This patronizing of the public's intelligence caused cynicism about all official news outlets, and later real anger – as, for instance, when reports down-playing air-raid damage and casualties were heard by actual survivors. Reports from the SD on public opinion often mentioned demands that they be told the truth – they were mature enough to cope with it. Unfavourable comparisons were even drawn with the British practice of discussing setbacks and difficulties more openly, since such material was often picked up and quoted in the German press.

Conversely, when the undeniable disaster at Stalingrad in January–February 1943 led to a sudden new tone of grim determination in propaganda broadcasts, the change from boastful optimism was too sudden, and the lack of any reassurance that there was a credible way forward to ultimate victory caused widespread despair.

Films
Cinema-going was very popular, and Goebbels took full advantage of propaganda newsreels and other morale-boosting material; mobile

Propaganda at the most basic level was not neglected. As the Allies closed in on the Fatherland, slogans began to be painted on suitable surfaces all over the country in an attempt to motivate the population to keep the faith and make ever greater efforts and sacrifices. Here – behind a heap of earth, rubble and household debris, complete with the tailfins of a bomb – a wall proclaims *Alles fur Deutschlands Sieg!* – 'Everything for Germany's Victory!'

cinemas were even provided for remote rural areas. Total cinema visits in 1939 were 624 million, and these rose to 1,117 million in 1943; the average person went to the cinema at least once a month. Between 1933 and 1945 the film industry produced 1,094 full-length features; of these some 48 per cent were comedies, 27 per cent melodramas, 11 per cent action adventures, and 14 per cent pure propaganda. Some 20 million people saw the 1940 anti-Semitic historical drama *Jud Suss*; and 27 million – more than a quarter of the population – saw the June 1942 musical romance *Die grosse Lieb*, the most popular film of the war. In 1943–44 huge resources were devoted to making the inspirational Napoleonic Wars epic *Kolberg*, released as late as January 1945.

Postal and telephone services

Postal, telegraph and telephone services, together with some technical aspects of radio broadcasting, were combined in the autonomous Deutsche Reichspost organization. The head of the Ministry of Posts (Reichspostministerium) held cabinet rank, and was assisted by an under-secretary of state and an administrative council of six members chosen by the cabinet. This Beirat der Deutschen Reichspost decided the principles governing the use of the services, the fixing of charges and the scale of employees' salaries; it was also responsible for the introduction of new and the suspension of existing services.

The ministry in Berlin was divided into seven departments: (1) internal and international postal services (2) telephones, telephone cables and telephone circuit networks; (3) telegraphs and circuit construction; (4) personnel; (5) accounting and buildings; (6) general organization, advertising, purchasing, and transport, and (7), radio and television (the latter irrelevant during the war years).

Greater Germany was divided into 38 areas, and the headquarters of the Berlin area was also the Central Office of the State Post (Reichspostzentralamt). This functioned under the direct orders of the minister and had the same status as the seven departments; its President controlled Greater Berlin services, and also advised the ministry on technical recommendations made by the research stations located at Berlin and Dresden. He was also responsible for co-ordinating all general administrative questions.

The other 37 Regional Directorates (Reichspostdirektionen) were each headed by a President, who was responsible for the execution and administration of all services in his area.

The Reichspost operated an extensive motor transport service which, though introduced primarily for the conveyance of mails, was also used for carrying passengers. This often provided the only means for

A female postal worker sorts a bundle of mail for a BDM girl acting as a postal auxiliary (see Plate E1).

The ability to keep in touch with family and friends was obviously even more important in wartime, and telephoning was often difficult after the air raids became widespread. As many post offices were destroyed, the Reichspost laid on special mobile offices in vehicles; people in bombed areas could send free, pre-printed message forms to give or ask for emergency news. Here customers queue at the service windows of a motorized 'Fahrbares Postamt'.

passengers and mails to reach rural districts not serviced by a railway. The Reichspost ran its own vehicle repair and maintenance services and fuel depots.

As early as October 1935 telephone users in Germany were divided into three categories:

(1) Persons requiring strict supervision by the Gestapo. This category included embassies, legations, consulates and newspaper correspondents; former politicians, many Jews, and other persons suspected of disaffection. Every word spoken over telephone lines could be automatically recorded on Dictaphone records.

(2) Persons not regarded as quite safe but at the time not sufficiently important to be placed under permanent supervision. This category extended to practically all Jews, to Protestant pastors and Roman Catholic priests.

(3) Those persons not judged of sufficient interest to fall into categories (1) or (2) but who were subjected to spot checks from time to time.

Between 1943 and 1945 the use of a telephone during air raid alerts was generally prohibited, and long-distance telephone calls were also restricted for a period following raids – at which times lines were anyway often cut by bomb damage.

THE AIR WAR AGAINST GERMANY

The black-out, and gas masks

By the outbreak of war the precautions against air raids in Germany, as in Britain, had been carefully considered, but could only be predicated on contemporary examples, e.g. in Spain and China. The inability of the RAF to launch immediate heavy attacks in 1939 caused a public sense of anticlimax, especially as the regime – in the person of Göring – famously boasted that such raids would never get through. The victories of 1939–40 also reassured the public that the war was almost won, and that they would never face the ordeals suffered by others at the hands of the Luftwaffe.

The crew of a Luftwaffe 8.8cm anti-aircraft gun practice their loading technique in an emplacement somewhere on the outskirts of a large town.

The fear that enemy night bombers could be guided to urban targets by house, street and vehicle lights preoccupied the authorities in all the combatant nations. A total public black-out was enforced as a matter of course; light-proof curtaining was required to cover the windows and door frames of domestic dwellings, and office buildings where people required indoor lighting at night. Street lighting was switched off, and motorists were required to cover all but a small slot on the glass of hooded headlights – this restriction applied to military and also public service vehicles such as trams, buses and trains. In the latter, blue-tinted interior lightbulbs often replaced white, or the bulbs were covered with black cloth. However, neither trolley-buses nor steam trains could be blacked out effectively: the overhead electric contacts of the former gave off blinding flashes of blue-white light; and the latter threw sparks out of their funnels, tracing their tell-tale movement along consistent lines.

As in Britain, vehicle accidents after dark, with resulting injuries and deaths, increased considerably, although the shortage of petrol helped to reduce the density of traffic. Kerbstones in built-up areas were painted white, as were bands around lamp posts and other street furniture – usually around the base and at head height. People walking outdoors were encouraged to wear light-coloured outer garments, and most wore buttonhole badges coated in luminous phosphorus paint. Battery-powered torches were required to use dark blue bulbs or to have the glass obscured with black or red paper. The black-out had other drawbacks, of course: in Germany as elsewhere, crime of all sorts

flourished under the cloak of darkness – burglary, street prostitution, robbery, rape and murder.

The fear of enemy gas attack was very real. A civilian pattern People's Mask had been designed and manufactured before the war, and was distributed to adults throughout Germany; special gas masks were also devised for wear by young children and by nursing mothers.

Summary of the bombing campaign, 1942–45

British air raids started in late 1939, but only on a small scale; damage and casualties were inconsequential, and the official media sneered at these puny efforts – pointless leaflet drops, and insignificant attacks on coastal targets by a couple of dozen aircraft at a time. From the beginning of heavy raids on German cities in spring 1942, however, the original air-raid precautions were revealed as largely irrelevant. The important factors were the inability of the air defences – searchlights, anti-aircraft guns, day and night fighters, and increasingly sophisticated radar – to prevent many hundreds of RAF night and later USAAF day bombers from reaching German cities and industrial targets during repeated raids. Obviously this huge subject can only be introduced briefly in the space available here. To summarize, then:

On 10 June 1945 the British Air Ministry stated that RAF Bomber Command had dropped 657,674 tons of bombs on Germany (the great majority during night raids on cities); and the total RAF/USAAF tonnage has been reported elsewhere as 2,697,473 tons. It is believed that about 50 per cent of the total Allied tonnage fell on residential

The Luftwaffe Flakartillerie were supplemented in the active air defence of the Reich by auxiliaries provided by a number of civil organizations. The rank and file of this crew in a 2cm light AA emplacement are factory workers of a so-called Heimat-Flak ('Home Anti-Aircraft') unit, parading for inspection by a Luftwaffe officer. The men wear Air Force issue steel helmets and waist belts with dark overalls; the black-on-yellow 'Deutsche Wehrmacht' arm band signifies that while on duty they were classed as members of the German Armed Forces.

Wearing dark blue field caps and pale working blouses and trousers, men of the TeNo (note 'Technische Nothilfe' cuff title, extreme right) pause in their efforts to search the rubble of crushed buildings.

areas, and about 12 per cent on industrial, transport and military targets. Some 305,000 Germans were killed and 780,000 injured during air raids, and nearly 2 million homes were destroyed.[4]

Despite rapid advances in scientific navigational aids, 'pinpoint' accuracy on specific industrial and other high-value targets was seldom achieved even by the USAAF daylight offensive. The RAF suffered such high casualties in early daylight raids that night-bombing was the only viable tactic, and by night targets could only be hit by dropping large numbers of bombs and relying as much upon luck as upon judgement or technology. From spring 1942, therefore, RAF Bomber Command deliberately targeted German cities, in order to destroy the morale of workers as much as the country's infrastructure, and to force Germany to withdraw fighter squadrons and anti-aircraft regiments from the fighting fronts to defend the Reich. The size, frequency and range of RAF raids steadily increased. The first heavy attack on a city, heralding the new policy adopted by Air Marshal Sir Arthur Harris, chief of Bomber Command, was on 28/29 March 1942 on Lübeck, where some 8,000 incendiary bombs caused serious fires and killed (according to official German figures) 295 civilians. The Nazis could no longer make light of the effects of RAF raids; and despite their own attacks on Allied cities since the beginning of the war, the Propaganda Ministry dubbed the British crews 'air pirates', 'gangsters' and 'terror flyers'.

The first 'thousand-bomber raids' on West German cities such as Essen and Cologne in the industrial Rhineland began in June 1943. A shocking new phase of the war for German civilians and emergency services opened on 24/25 July 1943; over four consecutive nights and

---

[4] For comparison: the populations of Germany and Britain were about 78 million and 48.5 million respectively. German bombing and V-weapon attacks on Britain killed some 60,600 civilians and injured about 86,200; about 460,000 households were made homeless. Total German civilian deaths from all Allied action during the war were about 2.05 million, with a slightly higher number injured. Air raid deaths were thus about 15 per cent of total fatalities – slightly more than the 300,000 German civilians believed killed by the Nazi regime itself. (John Ellis, *The World War II Data Book*, Aurum, 1993)

The city of Cologne in the Rhineland suffered terrible destruction. Raids began in 1940, but the first RAF 'thousand-bomber raid' of 30/31 May 1942 opened a whole new phase. Armed forces and civil defence manpower was summoned to assist in the damaged areas, mostly to dig into the ruins in search of survivors and casualties and later to clear the rubble. Here, a unit of soldiers wearing off-white drill/ fatigue uniforms and carrying shovels pass another group of exhausted rescuers.

three days, alternating RAF night and USAAF day raids on Hamburg, totalling about 3,000 sorties, caused a 'firestorm' which destroyed perhaps three-quarters of the city. At least 42,000 people were killed and 100,000 injured; about 225,000 individual dwellings were destroyed, with some 3,600 business premises; many thousands of the shocked survivors fled to the surrounding countryside to camp out, the emergency services collapsed, and appeals had to be broadcast for days afterwards for responsible officials to return to their duties.

Berlin had been bombed before, but the capital became the focus of a major offensive between November 1943 and April 1944, and the raids of November alone made 400,000 Berliners homeless. The year spring 1943–spring 1944 involved a total of around 75,000 RAF Bomber Command sorties; the see-saw war of tactics and countermeasures between attackers and defenders cost the RAF some 2,800 aircraft, and about seven times that many aircrew. In all, Bomber Command suffered some 55,000 casualties during the war, the highest proportion of any British miltary command. In mid 1944 a great deal of the effort was switched to preparation and support for the liberation of France; thereafter tactical targets and short-range daylight raids predominated for a while. The RAF returned in strength to the night skies over German cities that autumn, and the campaign culminated in the Dresden raids of 13/14 February 1945 – which killed perhaps as many civilians as the 1943 Hamburg raids. The USAAF also carried out many raids on German cities, apart from its better-reported attacks on industrial targets. By the end of the war 20 German cities and major towns were classed as being virtually destroyed, and 19 others – including Berlin – as severely damaged.

The effectiveness of the bombing campaign has been argued and disputed endlessly. In the most general terms, post-war studies have revealed that bombed factories and their workers showed extraordinary resilience, and that despite massive losses and difficulties industrial production of armaments and related output did not begin to fail until

In late October 1943 the Reich Ministry of the Interior disclosed that 102,486 persons had been killed in air raids on 12 German cities between 1 April and 25 October. These photos show the recovery of two of them.

RIGHT **The poignantly small remains on the stretcher are wrapped in a blanket by men of the German Red Cross, after recovery by Luftwaffe personnel.**

BELOW **The dead woman lying on a sheet is surrounded by men of the Luftschutzpolizei (note collar** *Litzen***, left, on a Luftwaffe-style** *Fliegerbluse***).**

the last six months of the war. Even then, the main causes were destruction of the transport network (manufacturing was highly decentralized) and loss of the sources of raw materials and fuel. Civilian morale was greatly depressed, and trust in the regime was almost destroyed, but not the will to resist – nor to seek revenge. Even in the worst months the German public pinned their hopes, enthusiastically, on the Nazis' promise that 'miracle weapons' of unprecedented power would soon be unleashed to devastate Britain.

FIRE DEFENCE

The national Feuerschutzpolizei (Fire Protection Police) was created in 1938 by absorbing the professional fire-fighters of about 90 of the larger towns. The FSP became a branch of the Ordnungspolizei, under the command of the higher Police authorities. A Kreisführer commanded all fire brigades in a Stadtkreis or Landkreis, a Bezirksführer in a Regierungsbezirk, and an Abschnittsinspekteur in a Wehrkreis (military district).

The smallest administrative area was the Wachbezirk, composed of several Schutzpolizei Reviere (Protection Police precincts); operational zones (Ausrückbereiche) for actual fire-fighting were determined independently according to tactical considerations. The usual operational unit called out in the first instance was the Zug of two or three fire engines, and the corresponding Zugwache (watch squad) of ten to 12 firefighters. In exceptional cases a larger Gruppe was called out, with the corresponding Gruppenwache. The commander (Kommandeur or Leiter) in charge of local Feuerschutzpolizei units directed fire prevention and fire-fighting, allotted the respective zones

Women fulfilled an important role in organizations such as the Fire Protection Police; they were capable of undertaking most of the tasks normally carried out by male personnel, many of whom had been drafted into the military. These posed photos of female volunteers seem to include subjects covering a carefully selected range of ages. Note the Police model helmet, of thinner steel than the Wehrmacht M1935, and identifiable by the sharply angled brim in front of the ears and the two circles of ventilation piercing. They display the two Police decals, and the hose crew have the FSP leather neck flap added. Note also the heavy overalls, with the FSP carmine-red Police eagle on an oval green-grey patch on the upper left sleeve.

of operation to subordinate units, and supervised organization and operations. He was responsible for administrative purposes to the Oberbürgermeister or Bürgermeister of the local authority.

The size of the Fire Protection Police depended upon the population of the city; in those with more than 870,000 inhabitants, or with harbour installations, numerous industries or large areas that presented particular fire hazards, the number and nature of the Wachen were determined individually. In cities with populations greater than 150,000, auxiliary Freiwillige Feuerwehren (Volunteer Fire Brigades), organized in tactical Gruppen, were established to supplement the Feuerschutzpolizei. In exceptional cases, where insufficient volunteers came forward for the Freiwillige Feuerwehren, compulsory Pflichtfeuerwehren were established. The strength of these auxiliaries was fixed at about four times the strength of the local regular Fire Protection Police.

Smaller communities were protected by Freiwillige Feuerwehren and, when voluntary enlistment fell short, by obligatory conscription into the Pflichtfeuerwehren of available males between the ages of 17 and 65. These men were considered as Hilfspolizei (Auxiliary Police). The lower ranks of fire brigade leaders – Truppmänner, Obertruppmänner and Haupttruppmänner – were appointed by the Ortspolizeibehörde, and the Wehrführer (brigade commander) by the Kreispolizeibehörde. In localities where both voluntary and compulsory brigades existed they comprised a single fire department under a unified command.

CIVIL DEFENCE

Definition of terms is important here: the German term 'air *protection*' (Luftschutz) covered not only air-raid precautions but also the fire service, bomb disposal, smoke screens, decoy sites and camouflage. The active measures – fighter aircraft, anti-aircraft (Flak) batteries, searchlights and balloon barrages – came under the heading of 'air *defence*'.

The State Air Protection League (Reichsluftschutzbund, RLB) was founded in April 1933, to train all householders in domestic air-raid precautions. This pre-dated the revelation that Germany had an embryonic air force in defiance of the 1919 Versailles Treaty; early in 1933 a 'Ministry of Air Travel' had been set up, with Hermann Göring at its head, and this ministry took effective control over all air protection and defence measures.

On 13 March 1935 it was announced that Göring had become Minister for Air and Commander-in-Chief of the new Luftwaffe, and a few months thereafter responsibility for air protection was taken over by the Air Ministry. This responsibility was shared as follows: policy and national direction of operations lay with the Air Minister and the Air Force High Command; local services were organized as part of the Order Police, under the Ministry of the Interior; and the RLB provided wardens and fire-watchers, and instructed the public. On 26 June 1935 the voluntary status of the RLB was cancelled, and it became obligatory for almost all able-bodied adults to play some part in air-raid precautions. (The membership of the RLB in 1938 was given as 12.6 million, and in April 1943 as 22 million.) Other government departments dealt with special aspects, e.g. the Ministry of Economics (through the State Group for Industry) controlled industrial air-raid precautions; and the state-controlled services (railways, post office, inland waterways and national motor highways) had their independent organizations.

Members of a Hitler Youth fire-fighting squad. All wear Police helmets and are dressed in khaki-brown uniforms with stand collars, shoulder straps of rank, and the triangular district badge (Gebietsdreieck) on the upper left sleeve, above the Hitler Youth armband. The boy on the extreme right displays the diamond-shaped *HJ-Feuerwehrabzeichen* on his left forearm; this badge was introduced in 1941 for youths who had successfully passed a fire service test.

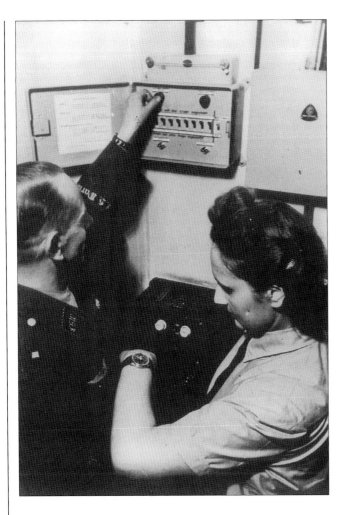

The Air Ministry and Air Force High Command controlled operations at regional level and above: most of the civil defence mobile reserve (SHD motorized battalions – see below), the Air Protection Warning Service (LSW – see below), shelter policy and lighting restrictions. The Ministry of the Interior, through the Police, controlled local SHD services in the towns – fire-fighting, rescue, first aid, veterinary services, and anti-gas measures – subject to policy dictated by Göring. Evacuation and post-raid services were the responsibility of the Nazi Party. The German civil defence organization fell into five main divisions:

(1) The national services organized and trained by the Luftwaffe. These comprised the Air Protection Warning Service (LSW), which tracked and reported raids in co-ordination with the Police, and controlled public warnings; bomb-disposal units; smoke troops, decoy sites and target camouflage. From 1942 onwards the main Air Protection mobile reserve units – the former SHD motorized battalions – also became a national service and part of the Luftwaffe as the Luftschutz Abteilungen (mot).

Sounding the 'all clear': a member of the LSW presses the button that electronically activates the sirens throughout his district. The responsibility for ordering all siren signals lay with the chief of the local Luftschutz headquarters; he held the only key to the siren control box, and he alone had access to it. The precise moment of sounding all 'general alarm' air raid warnings and 'all clear' signals was noted by the assistant. Note the 'L.S. Warndienst' left cuff title, the 'LSW' collar patch, and the Luftschutz badge worn on the right breast by this NCO equivalent (compare with Plate B2).

(2) Local services organized and trained by the Police: (a) warning services, and (b) from May 1942, the Air Protection Police (Luftschutzpolizei) – the former non-mobile SHD.

(3) The State Air Protection League (RLB) was responsible for educating and training the public and providing wardens and fire-watchers. It embraced both the Self-Protection Service (for residential areas), and the Extended Self-Protection Service (for business premises, institutions, places of entertainment, etc). It was not affiliated to the Party – although many of its prominent members were Nazi leaders – and kept clear of it until 1945. In March 1934 a law authorized the wearing of an RLB uniform.

(4) The services of major industrial concerns were organized and trained by the State Group for Industry under the Minister of Economics. Apart from the state-owned entities (see 5 below), industry as a whole was covered by the Factory Air Protection Service (Werkluftschutzdienst).

(5) Railways, post office and inland waterways were self-contained, and each was responsible for organizing and training its own civil defence services, which followed the same pattern as for major industry. These came directly under the authority of Göring, and co-operated with the local services as required.

In operations within a town the Police chief controlled entirely groups (2) and (3), and could call on groups (1), (4) and (5) for assistance.

Air raid warning signals

In the early part of the war only two signals were used on LSW sirens – the 'general alarm' and the 'all clear'. On the sounding of the general alarm all activity ceased, traffic stopped and industry halted.

As the frequency of raids increased changes became necessary to prevent loss of working hours. An elaborate system of confidential telephoned alerts to war industries, etc, gave 12-minute and six-minute warnings. Public warnings conveyed signals for 'small raid possible', 'immediate danger', 'pre-all clear' and 'all clear'. Information on the movements of enemy aircraft and the progress of raids was also broadcast from the end of 1942 onwards. There were in all seven forms of warning, of which five were public. It was laid down that only on a warning of the approach of more than three aircraft flying in formation, or more than ten not in formation, were people to go to the shelters.

Air Protection Police

The Luftschutzpolizei was formed in spring 1942 from the former mobile battalions of the Security & Assistance Service (Sicherheits u.Hilfdienst, SHD). The SHD was formed in 1935 under Police direction, as a civil defence service in 106 of the largest 'first category' towns and cities that were the most vulnerable to air raids. In 1940 a motorized SHD strategic reserve of three to four battalions was formed to provide reinforcement to towns under heavy attack; each town having an SHD transferred a quota of men to form the nucleus for these mobile battalions, which were self-supporting, well-equipped and capable of rapid transfer.

As a result of the first heavy attacks on Lübeck and Rostock in spring 1942 the air protection organization was overhauled; in April/May 1942 the SHD was renamed the Luftschutzpolizei (Air Protection Police), which provided the following local services: fire-fighting and decontamination; rescue and repair; first aid posts, first aid parties and ambulances; veterinary services, and gas detection services. The administration and training of the Luftschutzpolizei remained under the Order Police, although Göring was responsible operationally for this, as all other air protection services. The number of Air Protection Police allotted to a town was roughly in proportion to the population. The personnel were under Police discipline, lived in barracks, and wore a uniform similar to that of the Luftwaffe but with distinctive Police-style insignia.

It should be noted that the voluntary technical services – Technische Nothilfe (TeNo), the Todt Organization, the Evacuation Police, etc – were not part of the Air Protection Police, although they co-operated closely with it.

The mobile reserve battalions of the former SHD were transferred to the Luftwaffe and renamed Luftschutz Abteilungen (mot) or Motorized Air Protection Battalions; the number of battalions was also greatly increased. Their activities were mainly confined to fire-fighting, rescue and debris-clearance duties, with some decontamination and first aid work. They thus became part of the national rather than local services.

A mixed group of uniformed personnel help damp down smouldering rubble after a raid; among them Hitler Youth fire-fighters, RAD and RLB personnel can be made out.

Self-Protection Service

The Air Protection law of 26 June 1935 made participation in air-raid precautions compulsory for practically all able-bodied Germans. On 4 May 1937 a decree in application of this law laid down the services to be performed, the procedure for conscripting personnel, and the conditions of service.

This organization formed the first line of domestic defence against air raids. Its main functions were the equipping of communal cellar shelters and the performance of fire-watching duties under the direction of the house warden, under the operational orders of the chief of the Police precinct. The squads were trained, organized and led into action by the block warden, while the individual fire-watchers were controlled by the house warden – who was frequently a woman. In large 'first category' towns the Air Protection Police were available to reinforce the Self-Protection Service at any incident beyond its control. The organization had no obligation to report an incident immediately unless it was beyond their capabilities. In small towns and rural communities the service formed an 'air protection fellowship'; these, the Feuerwehren (Volunteer Fire Brigades), and – for rescue duties – local personnel provided by the TeNo, were the sole forces immediately available. Help could be sent from the nearest town when necessary.

Members of the Self-Protection Service were expected to supply their own clothing and equipment other than a respirator and steel helmet.

Extended Self-Protection Service

This service was established to cover those institutions, government offices, hotels and other communal buildings not large or important enough to the war effort to have a Factory Air Protection Service. It was administered and operated similarly to the Self-Protection Service, but with certain additional features, i.e. a leader-in-charge, control room for the premises, and simple rescue and first-aid equipment. Shelters had to be provided for employees. Training of leaders was carried out by the Police, and the leaders in turn trained their personnel. All other members forming the reserve groups were trained by RLB wardens on payment of the appropriate fees to the League.

Factory Air Protection Service

For the supervision of war production as well as air-raid protection, Germany was divided into industrial divisions, in each of which an Air Protection Leader was appointed; the division was sub-divided into regions, districts or smaller segments, each with an appointed leader. This service provided a rapid channel for information to each factory.

The Werkluftschutzdienst organization within an industrial concern resembled that of the local authority service (air protection leader, control room, fire-watchers, fire-fighting, decontamination and first aid squads, and – where a factory used animals – a veterinary section). The personnel were recruited from employees by the air protection leader, who himself was appointed by the Police. The works leader could in case of emergency call upon all persons within his sphere of responsibility or those in the vicinity to give temporary assistance to his squads. There were limitations on the number of times certain classes and age groups could be required to do duty in any one month. In many cases women employees were required to serve in all capacities. Those factories employing more than 100 people had to provide strong and mechanically ventilated shelters, which were subject to regular inspection. When the tempo of raids increased the types of shelters had to be revised, some factories going so far as to construct the multi-storied 'bunker' type. Training for key factory air protection personnel was given in a chain of independent schools, these leaders in turn training the factory employees.

If an incident in a factory was beyond the capabilities of the works squads and co-opted assistance, the local authority Police president would be asked for help; in many cases the town fire and other services would anyway be sent to help immediately information of an incident was received. The factory fire brigade was also at the disposal of the Police president, as this service was an official auxiliary unit of the town fire-fighting force.

Post-raid services

Arrangements were made in the first months of the war for the division of tasks between the appropriate Nazi Party functionaries and the local authorities. The Party was responsible for 'rest centres' and 'collecting posts'. The local authority provided an administration bureau where questions of billeting, feeding and care of air-raid victims were handled, in close co-operation with the rest centres. There were on average about five rest centres in each Police precinct, generally in school buildings. If a number of rest centres were destroyed, the Police then directed people to a collecting post – normally established in a church, theatre, cinema or other large building – to await evacuation.

Incidents were reported to Party officials either at the rest centre or at the district Party headquarters, and arrangements were then made for a meal to be provided for air-raid victims, who were in the meantime assembled by Party officials at rest centres or collecting posts. Women welfare workers were summoned to the various assembly points; if necessary, emergency quarters were thrown open to shelter those for whom local groups could not find more suitable accommodation. Local authority officials visited all points to confer with local group leaders over what further assistance was required.

It was stressed that the work of schools whose buildings were picked for rest centres should not be interrupted except in the case of unusually heavy raids. Storage of goods, bunks, etc, for use in centres had to be arranged so as not to interfere with school routine, and teachers were instructed in their use. The rest centres were only to open when the homeless could not be accommodated by relations, friends or neighbours. When shelter was needed for longer periods, the homeless were billeted or evacuated. Billets were supplied and controlled by the NS-Volkswohlfahrt (National Socialiest Welfare Organization), assisted by the NS-Frauenschaft (National Socialist Women's Association, NSF).

Nursing auxiliary of the NS-Schwesternschaft dispensing soup at an open-air feeding station. For air-raid survivors and emergency workers alike, food and drink were immediate essentials. The Party organized field kitchens – usually at large central locations such as city parks – which provided basic food for a few days. Reserved stocks of tinned produce were also opened up and distributed, and extra bonus food rations were made available to air-raid victims. In bombed areas, and more generally on special occasions such as Christmas, there was limited distribution of treats to raise morale – real coffee, chocolate, sweets and alcohol. Air-raid victims were given special entitlements to replace clothes and other essentials, but these predictably involved bureaucracy and delays.

Emergency feeding was carried out by the Party, or by the local authority if it had facilities for feeding large numbers.

Information concerning dead, injured and missing persons was obtained from the Police and a record was kept by the local authority; information about the whereabouts of people who had moved was kept by the Civilian Registration Office, which was situated at the Police station.

Evacuation

In order to avoid mass panic, controlled evacuation away from bombed areas was essential. The Party Gauleiter of each Gau determined the reception areas, arranged for transport and, in his capacity as State Defence Commissioner, gave the order to evacuate. The Party and the local authorities co-operated in pre- and post-raid evacuation; the local authority and the appropriate labour office agreed which classes of the community – in the light of the local labour supply – could or could not be evacuated.

In September 1940 it was announced by the Berlin authorities that parents who wished to evacuate their children to safe areas could apply for a state subsidy towards the cost. The scheme was voluntary, and available to all parents, rich or poor, who wished to evacuate their children. By 25 October some 62,000 children under the age of 14 had been evacuated from the capital, with a further 30,000 to follow, and Hamburg had evacuated 42,000. The reception areas were for the most part in Bavaria, Silesia and Thüringia.

Members of the NS-Volkswohlfahrt (NSV) were to be found on duty at main-line railway stations to provide assistance to the thousands of evacuees being moved by special trains away from the heavily bombed areas. Note the cap band, with Gothic letters 'NS' alternating with the NSV runic symbol.

All vacant dwellings or under-used spare rooms had to be registered with the housing department of the local authority, and on 10 October 1942 it was announced that all such dwellings were subject to compulsory requisition. A system of priorities would be used in the allocation of such premises to the homeless or evacuees.

In June 1943 a wholesale evacuation from the Ruhr took place – one million women, children and elderly people. This led, on 23 June, to the creation of a national agency for the provision of living quarters for refugees. The decree, signed by Martin Bormann, empowered a Housing Commissariat under Dr Ley to requisition for this purpose all flats and rooms in houses that were not fully occupied in the reception areas in Bavaria, Austria, central and eastern Germany, as well as Czechoslovakia and other occupied countries. In August 1943 the Berlin radio announced that over a million women, children, elderly and invalids were being evacuated from the capital to reception areas in Mark Brandenburg, East Prussia and Wartheland, in batches of thousands, by special trains. Similar evacuations had begun from Stettin. The *Kölnische Zeitung* wrote that a 'great migration is now in progress as the result of British and American bombing', and the *Frankfurter Zeitung* that 'the entire German homeland is threatened by terror attacks'. (The Munich press announced that the vicinity of Hitler's private residence at Berchtesgaden had been barred to all evacuees.)

Evacuations were unpopular with all concerned. Those in whose properties space was requisitioned for billets resented the intrusion, and the evacuees were cramped, uncomfortable, homesick and disoriented. Ill-feeling between classes, churches, and between town and country people was widespread; and it was believed that the burden of providing billets – like so many other hardships – was being avoided by the well-to-do and well-connected. Above all, evacuation completely disrupted family life – and in these hard times the family unit was about all most people had left to cling to for happiness and reassurance. Finding this intolerable, many refugee women defied the authorities and returned home, despite control of their ration cards in attempts to prevent this.

The destruction of homes by bombing aggravated an already serious pre-war housing shortage in Germany. After the economic depression of the late 1920s the years since 1933 had seen the Nazi economy devoted to re-armament. Before June 1941 it was reckoned that the country was already 6 million apartments short of what the population needed; by the beginning of 1944 the shortfall was an estimated 11 million dwelling units. The government built emergency housing for the bombed-out from 1943, on estate complexes, but these never approached the numbers needed.

A DAF band giving an open-air performance for factory workers during their break time.

PLATE COMMENTARIES

A1: *SA-Gruppenführer, 1939–43*
This senior officer commands one of the 29 regional Gruppen of the Sturmabteilungen; the red panel on his cap indicates Gruppe staff status, its silver lace and piping also show senior rank, and that of SA-Gruppenführer is identified by his collar patches. He is permitted to wear an 'honour pistol', although the SA was strictly an unarmed organization. The silver lace cuff rings, 4mm above 12mm, indicate – uniquely among Nazi uniforms – not a grade, but the year he joined the SA: this combination indicated 1929.

A2: *NSDAP-Dienstleiter*
The rank of this senior Nazi Party functionary in service dress is identified by the eagle and triple oakleaves on his collar patches, and their dark brown ground shows his appointment at the level of a Kreis or district. The lace and piping on his Party armband also indicate his level of function. The uniform colour – and general demeanour – of these Party officials led to their nickname of 'Golden Pheasants'. Distinct from appointments, there were no fewer than 29 Party 'ranks' between the Gauleiter and the humble 'aspirant leader' – the rank illustrated was the seventh down from Gauleiter.

A3: Fireman, Berlin *Feuerschutzpolizei*
This fire-fighter of the national Fire Protection Police displays on the left sleeve of his working overalls the Police national emblem in the carmine-red of the fire service, beneath a district designation. The distinctive Police helmet has a leather curtain attached under the rear to protect the neck from embers and water. His cased axe is attached to the broad fire-fighter's belt, with its steel spring clip and D-ring for ropes. (**Inset**) The decal worn on the right of the helmet, opposite the Police eagle shield shown on its left.

B1: Fireman, *Sicherheits u.Hilfsdienst,* winter 1941/42
The Security & Assistance Service (SHD) were conscripted civil defence squads who lived part-time in barracks, and enjoyed immunity from military call-up. The steel helmet is the civilian or 'RLB' model, of broad outline with a rib around the base of the skull; it has the RLB decal on the front, and is worn with an M38 gas mask. The uniform reflects the Air Ministry/Luftwaffe control of all national air-raid protection services. The green insignia include Gothic 'SHD' collar patches edged with green-and-white cord, green shoulder straps and (from December 1941) an armband with the name of the service in yellow Gothic script. An initial letter patch in different colours on the left forearm (hidden here, but see **inset**) identified each of the five specialist branches of the SHD – here 'F' for Feuerlösch in white on red, edged green.

B2: *LSW-Oberzugführer, Luftschutzwarndienst*
The Air Protection Warning Service (LSW) was the other important civil air protection branch, tracking raids and giving public warnings. Like the SHD, the LSW wore Air Force-type uniform and green insignia; the collar patches bear Gothic letters 'LSW', the narrow officer-style shoulder straps have inset green lines, and the green left cuff title has Gothic lettering *L.S.Warndienst*. The LSW emblem is worn by this officer on both his left upper sleeve and the crown of his Luftwaffe-style service cap.

B3: *Hauptluftschutz-Führer, Reichsluftschutzbund*
The State Air Protection League (RLB) supervised all civil defence training throughout Germany; members gave practical demonstrations, arranged lectures and presented film shows. The membership, of more than 20 million, was structured into 15 Länder groups, with each Gruppe divided into Ortsgruppen. The distinctive colour was violet, seen here on the rank collar patches; shoulder straps or cords were worn on the right only. This officer, in the distinctive RLB overcoat and with the League's dress dagger, is shown while collecting for the Winter Relief Fund (Winterhilfswerk des Deutschen Volkes).

The emblem of the RLB, worn as a white embroidered badge on the uniforms of the air protection services, and as a helmet decal in silver-grey on the thin steel civilian-model helmet worn by the SHD and Luftschutzpolizei, including auxiliaries. See Plate B1.

C1: *OT-Kameradschaftsführer, Organisation Todt, 1942–43*

The OT was created by the civil engineer Dr Fritz Todt, and built much of the Autobahn system and the German 'West Wall' defences on government contract. During the war OT Work Groups (Einsatzgruppen) worked as construction units throughout occupied Europe; the OT co-operated closely with numerous private firms as well as the Wehrmacht, and employed increasing numbers of foreign workers. Units were employed extensively throughout Germany in post-raid work, not only clearing rubble but also helping in rescue work. On his M1940 khaki tunic this junior leader's grade is shown by the bar across his shoulder straps (which are piped yellow, for the signals section) and two right sleeve chevrons; above these note his Flemish national shield. On his left sleeve are the OT junior ranks' armband, and a 'Blitz' signaller's badge; in his buttonhole is the ribbon of the War Merit Cross.

A studio portrait photo of a Werkschutzpolizei man. The distinctive arm badge worn above his rank chevron was the emblem adopted by the Factory Protection organization, and note the cap eagle bearing the same tilted swastika shield. The yellow arm band with a black eagle, indicating a person in state service, is worn butted down against the 'Werkschutz' cuff title. He also displays a Party membership badge, above the sword-and-swastika badge showing that he has completed SA pre-military training, and the ribbon of the War Service Cross in his buttonhole. The uniform itself and other insignia varied from employer to employer. See Plate D2.

C2: *Vormann, Reichsarbeitsdienst*

Units of the State Labour Service (RAD) were frequently pressed into post-raid rescue and clearance work. His field cap is tucked into his waist belt, and slung across his chest is an anti-gas cape inside its waterproof case. The M1935 RAD uniform bore no shoulder straps for conscript privates, whose rank was identified by the collar patches. The spade-shaped patch on the left sleeve bore battalion and company numbers – here, those of 2 Kompanie, 318 Abteilung, a unit of divisional district XXXI, Oberrhein.

C3: *TN-Vormann, Technische Nothilfe, 1941–42*

The Technical Emergency Service (TeNo), which was raised in September 1919 as a strike-breaking organization, was tasked with maintaining vital public services such as sewerage, gas, electricity and water supplies. Like all German uniformed organizations the TeNo had their own ranks and distinctive insignia (in their case in silver-grey on black), displayed here on the field-grey uniform worn when assisting the Wehrmacht. Those illustrated, specific to the period, are the cogwheel left collar patch of both the junior ranks of TN-Nothelfer and TN-Vormann, with the three-barred shoulder strap of TN-Vormann; unit numbers – a Roman above an Arabic numeral – were displayed on the right collar patch. The TeNo insignia worn on the field cap (**inset**) differed from the larger presentation on the left sleeve in that the eagle's head faced in the opposite direction. The black left cuff title bears the organization's name in silver Gothic lettering between silver edges.

Units of all three of the organizations illustrated on this plate were periodically issued with small arms and belt equipment.

D1: *DAF-Werkscharführer, Deutsche Arbeitsfront*

Members of the Party-controlled trade union organization had to buy their own uniforms. The Scharführer ranks, identified by sleeve chevrons and pale blue shoulder strap piping, approximated to shop stewards, and were only open to reliable Party members. (**Inset**) DAF metal badge on black diamond, worn on left sleeve.

D2: *Werkschutzpolizist*

The larger factories and other industrial and commercial concerns employed their own security guards and fire service personnel. Werkschutzpolizei clothing and details of insignia varied widely, since these were civilian companies; some wore standard types of grey or blue uniform with the cap and left sleeve badges authorized by the Air Ministry, and 'Werkschutz' cuff titles in various colours. Individual firms sometimes issued collar patches with their symbols, here that of Deutsche Lufthansa; and various marks of grade were worn, these three chevrons presumably identifying a senior NCO-equivalent. He is a Party member who has qualified from SA paramilitary training, and holds the War Merit Cross.

D3: *DRB railway official, Reichsbahndirektion Nürnberg, c.1943*

The insignia used by German State Railways (Deutsche Reichsbahn) officials went through several changes in 1933–45, and often display contradictions to official regulations. The collar patches and shoulder straps

Officer and other-ranks equivalents in the Deutsche Rote Kreuz in service dress, and a DRK sister in ward dress, travelling in a large rapid response vehicle. See also photograph on page 26, and Plate E3.

illustrated show the system worn from February 1942; they identified pay grade groups – in this case, groups 8 and 7a. This left sleeve badge was introduced in September 1941, replacing a short-lived system of cuff titles. Below the gold-yellow eagle on the black patch is lettering 'RBD' (for Reichsbahndirektion, his department of function) 'Nürnberg' (for his railway division).

E1: Female postal worker, *Deutsche Reichspost*

With the majority of men either in the forces or engaged on essential war work, German women were encouraged to replace them on the railways, with tram and bus companies and the postal service. With her civilian blouse and shoes this woman wears a simple two-piece dark blue uniform, and the DRP peaked cap piped in orange and bearing full insignia. Women who were not fully qualified were supposed to wear a peakless beret bearing only the upper eagle of the cap insignia. The only jacket insignia is a left arm badge showing a yellow eagle between the words 'Deutsche' and 'Reichspost'. She carries mail in the large black leather satchel.

E2: DRB railway conductress, 1941–42

She wears a black uniform over a civilian sweater. The insignia include pre-1942 collar patches showing the DRB single-winged wheel; and, on her lapel, the *Kriegshilfsdienstabzeichen* (War Auxiliary Service Badge). This was introduced in July 1941 for girls who had completed a further six months' service in support of the war effort after their six months' basic service with the RAD/wJ (Reichsarbeitsdienst der weibliche Jugend – National Labour Service for Young Women).

E3: *DRK-Anwärter, Deutsche Rote Kreuz*

Assisting with air-raid casualties, this middle-aged medical orderly is equipped with an M1916 steel helmet with DRK decal (see **inset**), military issue medical orderly's belt pouches, the DRK 'hewer' sidearm, and slung bags with extra dressings. When the Nazis came to power the organization, ranks and insignia of the German Red Cross (DRK) were altered to reflect National Socialist control and a complex new structure. The slate-grey M1937 uniform bore dove-grey collar patches with a red enamel cross for all male ranks; this basic rank showed only dove-grey piping around the shoulder straps. The duty armband is white with the red Geneva cross between black lettering 'Deutsche/ Rote/ Kreuz'. His medal ribbon bar marks his World War I service and a recent award of the War Merit Cross.

F1: *Luftwaffe Flakwaffenhelferin*, winter 1943/44

The Female Anti-Aircraft Auxiliary uniform was Luftwaffe blue-grey: an M1943 peaked field cap, a single-breasted, fly-fronted, hip-length jacket with two patch skirt pockets, long trousers tucked into rolled socks, and ankle boots. In many cases female clothing was unavailable and male issue was handed out; under her greatcoat this girl wears a waist-length blouse cut down from a man's four-pocket tunic and altered to button to the left. The armshield of the Female AA Auxiliaries (**inset**) was worn on the right sleeve of jackets and coats; the single chevron on the left sleeve is that of this rank, in the sequence worn from July 1941 to June 1944 by all types of Luftwaffe female auxiliaries.

While perhaps peripheral to life on the Home Front, the female auxiliary branches of the armed forces must be described here briefly (see also under Plate H2, below).[5] Women in uniform served alongside the Heer, Kriegsmarine and Luftwaffe in various clerical, administrative, domestic and other support roles, and with the air defence system; but their organization was hesitant and on an *ad hoc* basis, originally as a voluntary option for members of the female RAD/wJ labour service.

The Luftwaffe recruited female auxiliaries for its Flugmeldedienst (Aircraft Reporting Service), which was

---

[5] For much fuller details of, among others, the uniformed Wehrmacht female auxiliary services, see MAA 393: *World War II German Women's Auxiliary Services*

absorbed in February 1941 into the Luftwaffen-achrichtenhelferinnen (Female Air Force Signals Auxiliaries). There were also Luftschutz Warndienst Helferinnen (Female Air Protection Warning Service Auxiliaries), and, as in the other armed services, Stabshelferinnen. The Luftwaffe Flakhelferinnen were not officially formed until October 1943, but anti-aircraft auxiliaries had previously volunteered from the RAD/wJ. Typically, these women manned searchlight batteries, barrage balloons and fire control equipment, although their employment in gun crews was authorized in the last months of the war.

F2: BD-Mädchen, Bund Deutsche Mädel, winter 1939/40
A member of the League of German Girls – the female equivalent to the Hitler Youth – in typical pre-1940 winter uniform: a four-pocket suedette jacket (*Kletterweste*) and dark blue Melton cloth skirt, with a white blouse, black necktie and leather slipknot. Her left sleeve insignia are, from top to bottom, the regulation triangular black district name-patch with silver-grey edging and Gothic lettering; the diamond-shaped HJ organization badge; and a special Gothic '*Landdienst der HJ*' cuff title in silver-grey on black. This indicates that she is undertaking a one-year period as a voluntary agricultural labourer.

F3: HJ-Oberkameradschaftsführer, Luftwaffenhelfer-Hitler Jugend
From January 1943, Hitler Youth boys aged 15 or older began to be called up to serve as auxiliaries in any branch of the Luftwaffe that required them; many were employed in the air defence of the Reich, helping to man the flak batteries that ringed the larger towns. Their official designation – Luftwaffenhelfer-Hitler Jugend (LwH–HJ) – was shortened for convenience to Luftwaffenhelfer, but they were more commonly known simply as Flakhelfer. This lad is shown wearing their distinctive blue-grey uniform of single–button cap, two-pocket field blouse, and trousers of a cut resembling those of armoured troops. The Hitler Youth

armband and cap badge are displayed. The triangular light-blue-on-black breast badge identified the LwH-HJ, as did the light blue piping on the shoulder straps bearing his rank insignia. Pinned to his pocket is the *Flak Kampfabzeichen der Luftwaffe* (Air Force Anti-Aircraft Battle Badge), showing that his unit has seen active service.

G1: Bzp-Unterzugführer, Bahnschutzpolizei, c.1942
The Railway Protection Police wore a unique light blue-grey uniform with dark blue-grey collar and cap band, and silver and silver-grey 'metal and lace'. The wreath around the cap cockade incorporated a double-winged wheel motif, also seen on the belt buckle. The black and white Police-style NCO shoulder straps of this rank have silver distinctions: a single pip, below a unit number, below a double-winged wheel. The black collar patch of rank has broad and narrow double edging and a double-winged wheel motif above a single pip. The Bzp's distinctive left sleeve eagle is very similar to the first-pattern SS-Verfügungstruppe type. The colouring of the M1941 cuff titles, with Gothic lettering '*Bahnschutzpolizei*', varied for groups of ranks; this silver-on-black style was for the junior group, from Bzp-Anwärter to Stellv. Bzp-Gruppenführer.

G2: Oberwachtmeister, Schutzpolizei des Reiches, c.1942
This Protection Police NCO, of equivalent rank to an Army Unterfeldwebel, wears everyday undress uniform in his city precinct station. The field cap, of Luftwaffe cut, has the silver-grey Police national emblem on black backing, and (from this year) piping in Police-green *Truppenfarbe* around the top edge of the flap. The *Waffenrock* tunic is in the distinctive Police green-grey with dark brown collar and cuff facings; these, and the front edge, are piped in Police-green. This colour is also displayed on the collar *Litzen*; and it edges the brown cord shoulder straps, outside the silver cords flecked with black chevrons, which identify senior NCO status. On the left sleeve the Police national emblem is worked in Police-green with a black swastika; the district title – here '*Köln*' for Cologne – is embroidered in an arc above the eagle. The belt buckle shows the wreathed mobile swastika of the Police; the silver rune patch below his pocket identifies simultaneous membership of the SS; blue long-service ribbons are pinned above the pocket, and that of the War Service Cross is sewn into his second front buttonhole.

G3: National staff member, NS-Frauenschaft
The National Socialist Women's Organization was the women's affiliate of the Nazi Party. It engaged in welfare and indoctrination work for the Party at all levels, but in particular

Young girls of the BDM working on a farm at harvest time – see Plate F2. The Nazis' general attitude to the female population can be gauged from Hitler's statement that 'in the education of women, emphasis must be laid primarily on physical development. Only afterwards must consideration be given to the spiritual values, and lastly to mental development.' However, there was no doubt that German farmers needed all the hands they could get: in 1939 the Reichs Food Minister admitted that since 1933 the agricultural sector had lost 400,000 workers.

This woman has been identified elsewhere as a Police auxiliary; she in fact serves, more specifically, with the Fire Protection Police as a team leader – note that she carries a long-hafted axe slung. She wears a Police-green field cap with the Police national emblem in silver-grey on black, repeated in FSP carmine-red on a green-grey patch on the sleeve of her heavy protective overalls.

at those of Ortsgruppe, Zell and Block; in 1942 it counted about 6.2 million members. Its basic function was to instruct and advise German women in what the Party called 'Volkswirtschaft' – domestic economy, the running of an efficient, economic home – on what it termed 'the Household Battlefront'; however, during the war it got involved in many other supportive welfare activities. The means employed were exhibitions, lectures, courses, instructional films, and the publication and distribution of leaflets and the journal *German Domestic Economy*. Paid leadership cadres were responsible for work at senior levels of the pyramid of local Party organization, from Gau downwards to Kreis and Ortsgruppe. They wore a blue-black civilian suit with a matching fedora hat and white blouse; a silver national emblem on black backing was worn on the upper left sleeve; left cuff titles identified districts, and the national leadership staff wore a '*Reichsfrauenschaft*' title. The enamel triangular NSF badge was worn on the left breast below the Party badge, with various coloured edgings indicating the level of leadership (see **inset**); these are reported as yellow (national leadership), red (Gau), black (Kreis) and light blue (Ortsgruppe). The actual individual leader at each level had a light grey outer edging, as illustrated inset for the Gau-level badge.

H1: Volkssturmmann, 1945

This conscripted Home Guard was divided into four classes or levies; the majority of over-age men served in battalions of Levy I and II, respectively available for duty anywhere in their Gau or their Kreis – the latter being made up of men whose war work was considered too important to call them up until the threat was very local.[6] They often received no uniforms beyond the armband (**inset**); what was issued tended to be a rag-bag of anything available – this man has been relatively lucky to receive an Army helmet and greatcoat and Luftwaffe trousers. Weapons and minimal field equipment were equally

6 For full details, see Warrior 110: *Hitler's Home Guard: Volkssturmmann, Western Front, 1944–45*

heterodox, but this elderly man is training with a Panzerfaust – the use-and-throw-away anti-tank rocket projector that was available in large numbers late in the war.

H2: Nachrichtenhelferin, Nachrichten Dienst des Heeres

This Army Female Signals Auxiliary has just been awarded the War Merit Cross with Swords 2nd Class, and holds the paper citation in her hand. She wears the original double-breasted grey tunic and skirt, and a male field cap with yellow signals *Waffenfarbe* piping at the crown and the front of the flap. The Army national emblem is worn on the cap flap and the right breast; the 'Blitz' badge of a qualified signaller on the left of the cap, the left sleeve and as a tie brooch; and a Gothic black-on-yellow title '*NH des Heeres*' on the left cuff.

Hitler and other leaders were adamant that German womanhood should not be 'militarized'. The first crack in this wall was made by the need for large numbers of non-combatant personnel in the Army administrations of occupied countries. In October 1940 the Nachrichten-helferinnen were formed; they blazed a trail for the Betreuungshelferinnen (Female Welfare Auxiliaries), women transferred from the German Red Cross in October 1941. (In April 1941 the Navy also began to recruit female auxiliaries.) Stabshelferinnen (Female Staff Auxiliaries) and Wirtschaft-shelferinnen (Female Economics Auxiliaries) followed in 1942. In December 1941 a law introduced the concept of compulsory service in the Wehrmacht auxiliary branches for women aged 18 to 40, but conscription was never very widely enforced. For most of the war the bulk of auxiliaries remained volunteers, who found the prospect of travel, responsibility and the glamour of a uniform (only actually authorized when abroad) more attractive than the constraints of life at home. Women serving with the armed forces were not permitted to be armed, even to protect themselves.

H3: HJ-Rottenführer, HJ-Streifendienst, 1944–45

Specially selected from reliable older teenagers of the HJ, the Hitler Youth Patrol Service formed units whose original task was to police the Hitler Youth itself. They sometimes found themselves in fights with 'anti-social elements' such as the Edelweiss Pirates; but during the last stages of the war they became an armed body, to assist the Police and the SS in rounding up escaped prisoners of war, foreign workers or bailed-out Allied aircrew, or indeed to arrest anyone suspected of resisting the regime. They were identified by their left cuff title (**inset**) and, when on duty, by a special gorget. They were trained to use small arms and carried rifles when on duty. This boy wears dark blue HJ winter uniform, with HJ cap badge, breast badge, armband and belt dagger; shoulder straps of rank; and the usual yellow-on-black triangular district patch (*Gebietsdreieck*) on his left sleeve.

INDEX